HOBSON'S

Introduction by E. R. Wood. A rich _____
timid and backward lad is married, somewhat against his will, to his
boss's efficient and determined daughter. Under her influence he
develops in ability, confidence and authority until he takes over the
business from the old tyrant, Henry Hobson, and that strange marriage
matures into an affectionate partnership.

THE HEREFORD PLAYS

General Editor: E. R. Wood

Harold Brighouse

Hobson's Choice

A LANCASHIRE COMEDY IN FOUR ACTS
with an Introduction and Notes by
E. R. WOOD

HEINEMANN EDUCATIONAL BOOKS

Heinemann Educational Books Ltd
Halley Court, Jordan Hill, Oxford OX2 8EJ

OXFORD LONDON EDINBURGH MELBOURNE
SYDNEY AUCKLAND SINGAPORE MADRID
IBADAN NAIROBI GABORONE HARARE
KINGSTON PORTSMOUTH NH (USA)

ISBN 0 435 22120 5

Hobson's Choice was first published by Samuel French Ltd

First published in *The Hereford Plays* 1964
Reprinted 1966, 1967, 1968, 1970, 1972 (twice),
1973, 1974, 1976, 1977, 1978, 1982, 1983, 1985,
1986 (twice), 1987, 1988

Printed in Great Britain by
Richard Clay Ltd, Bungay, Suffolk

INTRODUCTION

HAROLD BRIGHOUSE was born at Eccles, in Lancashire, in 1882 and died in 1958. He was educated at Manchester Grammar School, which he left just before he was seventeen to go into the textiles export business. In the evening when he was not working overtime or studying cloth construction at a technical school or taking lessons in commercial Spanish, he went to the theatre as often as he could. Manchester then had several theatres and music halls. When at twenty he moved to a London office, he had his evenings free for theatre-going, and became an enthusiastic 'gallery first-nighter'. He saw the early productions of a famous season of plays at the Court Theatre in Sloane Square under the management of Harley Granville-Barker and J. E. Vedrenne, who between 1904 and 1907 launched the Repertory Movement in Britain and stimulated a theatrical renaissance.[1] Brighouse tells in his autobiography, *What I Have Had*, of the excitement of those evenings:

> It wasn't, even as galleries went, comfortable. You sat on coconut matting over concrete, and your back was dug into by the knees of the man behind you. But the discomfort made you feel

[1] The principal achievement of the Court Theatre was to present over thirty new plays by authors then little-known or rarely played, including Ibsen, Shaw, Galsworthy, Masefield and Granville-Barker himself. Half-a-century later history has been repeated at the same theatre (now called the Royal Court), where the English Stage Company has given a first hearing to John Osborne, Arnold Wesker, N. F. Simpson, John Arden and many others, and introduced English audiences to the work of foreign dramatists such as Ionesco, Sartre, Brecht, Frisch, Genet, Beckett, Albee and Arthur Miller.

the more that you were doing something for art, and in the intervals you discussed whether the properest thing for Granville-Barker was to knight him or to erect a statue to him in Sloane Square.

From this and other 'voracious playgoing' (as Brighouse described it) he unconsciously learnt the elements of play construction. 'It was,' he wrote, 'my rich, random, unpremeditated first apprenticeship to playwriting.'

Brighouse's first success was the one-act play *Lonesome-Like*, in his opinion his best one-acter, and always among the most popular. His first full-length play, *Dealing in Futures*, was presented by the Glasgow Repertory Company in 1909. From then on he earned his living as a writer; in the next twenty years he wrote fifteen full-length plays and eight novels; he worked for the *Manchester Guardian* as a theatre critic and reviewer; in all he wrote over fifty one-act plays, many of which are still being performed by amateurs and being reprinted in collections. *Hobson's Choice* was first produced in America in 1915. When it was brought to war-time London the following year and presented mainly in daily matinées because of the fear of air-raids after dark, it ran for 246 performances. It is still frequently performed by repertory companies and by amateurs: it has been broadcast five times in the past year; it has been triumphantly filmed; and it has now taken its place in the repertory of the National Theatre.

Brighouse was the most successful of the Manchester School of dramatists[1], who were associated with the repertory company established in 1907 at the Gaiety Theatre there. Miss A. E. Horniman, inspired by the achievements of Granville-Barker at the Court Theatre in London, already referred to, provided the money to found repertory theatres in Dublin, Manchester and Liverpool. These regional theatres encouraged

[1] The other well-known writers were Stanley Houghton (author of *Hindle Wakes*) and Allan Monkhouse (author of *Mary Broome* and *The Conquering Hero*).

plays by local authors about local life. The Manchester School showed that Lancashire people made good material for drama and Lancashire speech could enrich the quality of stage dialogue. The enthusiasm of Manchester people for their theatre did not last, and in 1921 the Gaiety became a cinema, but the English Theatre had gained much from the enterprise and generosity of Miss Horniman. When Harold Brighouse at the age of seventy looked back on what he had had from life, he mentioned first Miss Horniman's Company. But for her there might have been no *Hobson's Choice*.

Hobson's Choice, a traditional comedy

What are the qualities that have made *Hobson's Choice* a classic of the English Theatre? Much of its quality is in its universality. It is at the same time a period piece and a play for all time; geographically it is firmly set in Lancashire, and it gains greatly in truth and zest from its setting; yet it is about people everywhere.

The play's events are dated in Victorian times, but its ideas and attitudes were in the air a generation later when it was written and performed. One of its themes is the right of women to determine their own lives, a claim already voiced in the theatre by Ibsen[1], Shaw[2] and Granville-Barker[3]. This linked with another theme of the early years of the century: the rebellion of the younger generation against parental tyranny. Neither theme is alive today in quite the same way as fifty years ago, but we can still be caught up in the basic fable: a conceited and self-centred old windbag is deflated, while a victim of his despotism, 'a backward lad', grows to his full potentialities, marries the boss's daughter and takes over his business.

The fall of Hobson is in the tradition, dating from Roman

[1] *A Doll's House* was first seen in England in 1881.
[2] *Man and Superman* was written 1901–3.
[3] *The Marrying of Ann Leete* (1899).

times, of classical comedy, in which a main character incurs the disapproval of the theatre audience because of his anti-social qualities, such as the arrogance of Malvolio, the empty bragging of Pistol, or the hypocrisy of Tartuffe or Joseph Surface. Classical comedy also tends to take the part of the young against their elders. After exposing the faults that make the character difficult to live with, comedy gives the audience the satisfaction of seeing him laughed at and pulled down a peg or two. Hobson can be played as such a figure of traditional comedy: though at first he appears a man of consequence, he is seen by the younger generation as a despot ripe for downfall in the household, in his business, and even in the 'Moonraker's' parlour.

Since comedy exposes the follies that are departures from socially-desirable behaviour, one character at least must set a standard of right and common-sense. In *Hobson's Choice* it is Maggie who sets that standard, by which we may judge the other characters. She is not only the scourge of her father's folly; she is also a corrective to the silliness of her sisters and their young men – the snobbery, the business inefficiency, the trivial thinking about marriage, and the false priorities in setting up a home. In the end we see the three sisters put to the test, in the folk-tale scene of a father inviting each daughter in turn to say what she will do for him; here Maggie triumphs because she has not only the most sense, but also the best heart.

Just as Maggie shows up by her soundness the inadequacies of the other women, so Will Mossop is in time revealed as a solid standard by which we may measure the other young men. We can see who will be thought the most of at the bank in ten years' time; we may expect, too, that the strange, un-romantic marriage, built on belief in each other, and maturing into genuine affection, will be the most durable of the three. For the play is more than an exposure of folly and pretension and a celebration of common-sense: the relationship between Maggie and Will brings out the best in both and reminds us of some words of G. K. Chesterton: 'A marriage is neither an ecstasy nor a slavery: it is a commonwealth.'[1]

Characterization

Hobson's Choice has a firm foundation, then, of traditional comedy, but it has a rich spirit and atmosphere of its own. Classical comedy tends to be cold, even cruel, and its characters to be types or caricatures. This is not true of *Hobson's Choice*. 'In play writing,' Brighouse wrote, 'I put character first'; and he clearly took delight in creating rounded human beings. Thus Hobson is much more than a mere butt of comedy; the part offers opportunities for sympathetic playing; we can enjoy his gusto and his crusty eloquence at the beginning, and feel sorry for him (as Will Mossop does) at the end. Sir Michael Redgrave's playing of the part in the National Theatre production suggests a hint of a small-town King Lear unkindly treated by his thankless daughters.

Maggie too is much more than the efficient organizer of the fortunes of Mossop and Hobson. She is one of the great creations of the Twentieth Century Drama. When she makes her bargain with Will Mossop, 'I want your hand in mine and your word that you'll go through life with me for the best we can get out of it,' we are most aware of the hard, practical side of her nature, which makes her wary of sentiment which may stray into sentimentality. But the actress playing the part should look for early signs of emotional warmth. When Maggie takes one of Mrs Hepworth's flowers to press in her Bible as a keepsake, we have a foretaste of her words at the end of the play about the ring, in which genial wisdom transcends mere common-sense:

'I'll wear your gold for show, but that brass stays where you put it, Will, and if we get too rich and proud we'll just sit down quiet and take a long look at it, so as we'll not forget the truth about ourselves.'

[1] In his book on George Bernard Shaw.

There follows a touching moment of inarticulate affection that is worth an age of romantic talk, and this is true to Maggie's nature and to Will's.

Will Mossop presents an interesting problem to the actor, for he must greatly develop. At the beginning he is described as 'not naturally stupid, but stunted mentally'. As he pops up out of the trap-door in the stage (the very action is a cue for laughter in the theatre) he is a figure of fun, wincing when a person says 'take that', because he expects 'that' to be a blow, unable to read a visiting card, bobbing down into the cellar 'like a rabbit'. Throughout the first half of the play he is a well-meaning but slow-witted underling, comic because he is out of his depth. We see him grow from this abject creature to become the strongest man in the play. The comedy then lies in the surprise and incongruity of this same man now dominating his surroundings. Yet at his most masterful he never ceases to be likeable. As he shows out his routed sisters-in-law who once patronized him, he says, 'Nay, come, there's no ill-will,' and when he has scored his final victory over Hobson he says, 'He's crushed-like, Maggie. I'm afraid I bore on him too hard.' He can assume an air of great self-assurance, and he knows very well what he wants and where he is going, but he is still modest enough to be amazed at his own boldness and to give Maggie most of the credit for his good fortune.

The characters of Maggie and Will are created in depth. The more we see of them the better we know and like them. The minor characters are naturally shallower in conception, but they are not stock theatrical types (except perhaps the Scottish doctor) and every one offers scope for acting.

Construction

Harold Brighouse admired theatrical craftsmanship in others and learnt and practised it himself. There is a tendency now-adays to despise the 'well-made play', as if shaping the material to achieve full theatrical effect must necessarily kill truth and sincerity. But play-making is a skill; 'well-made' plays are meretricious only when the technique exploits material which is false or shoddy. *Hobson's Choice* is well-constructed according to the tradition of its time. That tradition at its best is a satisfying blend of naturalism and artifice. Every effort is made to create the illusion of real people talking about real problems and situations, but the success of the illusion conceals the skill with which the scenes are contrived.

Each act of *Hobson's Choice* has its shape, and can be sub-divided into scenelets, each having its own point, rhythm and climax. Notice the economy of the opening dozen lines, which give to the audience, naturally and as if incidentally, necessary information: that Hobson drinks more than is good for him (a fact that assumes great importance later); that his daughters are restive under his rule; and that Alice has a young man, who forthwith arrives. Here begins a comic scene in which Maggie makes Albert Prosser pay heavily for a very brief encounter. The theatre thrives on clashes of wills and wits, and here is a vivid demonstration of Maggie's strength. The incident is deliberately shaped in three stages: Albert at first hopes to get away jauntily at the cost of a pair of bootlaces, then he finds himself buying new boots against his will, and is finally swept into leaving his old boots for repair. As Maggie firmly shows him out, his discomfiture is complete, for he has been allowed only five words with Alice. There is a little coda to the scene, rounded off by Maggie's shrewd comment on courting: 'See that slipper with a fancy buckle to make it pretty? Courting's like that. All glitter and no use to nobody.' Maggie's view of romantic love is of the essence of the play.

A new movement comes with the entrance of Hobson – a new set of clashes. He first lectures Alice and Vickey on 'uppishness'; he then tells Maggie she is too old to expect a husband. Maggie's reaction is quiet, but when he has gone she takes action to prove him wrong. But first we have the short scene with Mrs Hepworth, which has a double purpose: it

prepares us for Mrs Hepworth's backing of Maggie later, and
it presents to us for the first time our hero Will Mossop at his
least impressive. Everything so far is preparation for the future,
but this is not obvious in the theatre.

For stage purposes Hobson needs someone in whom he can
confide, so that the audience know what he is thinking, both
now and later. This is the function of Jim Heeler, but Brighouse manages to make him a real character, amusing and
shrewd.

We are now ready for the main scene, in which Maggie
'woos' the reluctant Willie. This is written with an acute sense
of theatre, exploiting the paradox (by the standards of conven-
tional love-scenes) of the situation. Will is comic in the slow-
ness of his realization of what Maggie is after and the
incongruity of his reactions, his fear of what Mrs Figgins will
say and his relief at Maggie's countermeasures. Brighouse
smoothly contrives the appearance of Ada in person. If there
is a touch of harshness in the ousting of Ada, we must agree
that she would never do for Will, even without her mother
in the background. There remains the question, full of dramatic
tension, of what Hobson will say when he hears the news. The
audience is not kept waiting: Hobson comes in to dinner, and
the conflict comes to full intensity. So the act ends in the
splendid climax in which Willie, provoked by Hobson's blow,
defiantly kisses Maggie and adds, 'If Mr Hobson raises
up that strap again, I'll do more. I'll walk straight out of
shop with thee and us two 'ull set up for ourselves.' The
curtain comes down on Maggie's line: 'Willie! I knew you
had it in you, lad.' But Willie is not yet won, and has only
started to grow.

The ensuing acts show the same kind of scene-shaping, each
scene having its own tone and its climax. Act II ends with
Willie and Maggie setting out to the church, but although
Willie says he is 'resigned' and ready to 'toe the line', he cannot
yet be wholly relied on: Maggie does not trust him to take the

ring. Act III shows Hobson in decline, and then ends on the wedding night with Willie being led off by the ear. This moment runs the risk in performance of becoming too farcical, but it is an example of the larger-than-life incident that can be acceptable in the theatre. The theatre, after all, is theatrical, and this comic effect rounds off the act and gives a visual impression of Willie as a captive, not yet reconciled to his good fortune.

The last act is quite different in tone. Two strands of the plot – the Hobson element and the Willie element – have to be completed and tied up. The tables are finally turned on Hobson when he has to accept stiff but not unreasonable terms dictated by the 'backward lad' of the early scenes. The anti-romantic wooing is over; Maggie no longer needs to drag Willie by the ear. The marriage is no longer a joke, but a 'commonwealth'. The whole play has led up to a heart-warming conclusion, which is a triumph of character-building, technical sureness, and unpretentious comment on human relationships. The play would not have lived for half-a-century without its craftsmanship.

Language

An important feature of the regional drama to which *Hobson's Choice* was an outstanding contribution was the expressiveness of local speech. At the beginning of the century the theatre became aware of the eloquence and poetry of the Irish, the craggy toughness of the Scots, the warm country drawl of the Devon farmer, the quick-witted banter of the Cockney. Radio and television plays today are full of the accents of Belfast, Liverpool, Glasgow, the Black Country or London's East End, which contribute to the energy and realism of the dialogue. We need to distinguish between *dialect*, which includes words and turns of phrase that are peculiar to a particular region, and *accent*, which is merely the way in which the language is pronounced locally.

Looking closely at *Hobson's Choice*, we shall not see much enrichment of the English language by dialect. There are a few Northern idiosyncrasies, such as saying, 'You'll come, *so what* he says' (meaning *no matter what*); *none* for *not*, as in 'You'll none rule me'; *nowt* for *nothing*; *and all* as an emphatic extension, as in 'He is an' all'. The second person singular (*thee* and *thou*) occurs occasionally, but not at all consistently; and the definite article *the* is reduced to *t'* or disappears altogether. But what *Hobson's Choice* gains from Lancashire speech is not so much the vocabulary as the character of the things said, a kind of forthright plainness that is in tune with Lancashire people. Hobson's hard-headed suspicion of subtlety and cleverness is expressed in his rough aphorism, 'Honest men live by business and lawyers live by law.' When Vickey reproves Maggie for taking a brass ring out of stock for her wedding ring, all Maggie's Lancashire sense is in her reply, 'They're always out of someone's stock.' Lines like these need to be spoken with a Lancashire accent, which sounds strong and free from affectation. The final exchange of faltering endearments between Will and Maggie could hardly be translated into sophisticated Kensington speech. Any Northerner knows how much simple feeling can be conveyed in 'Eh, lad!' and the answer, 'Eh, lass!', and what a world of meaning can be expressed in the last words of the play, 'Well, by gum!'

Hobson's Choice

CHARACTERS

ALICE HOBSON
MAGGIE HOBSON
VICKEY HOBSON
ALBERT PROSSER
HENRY HORATIO HOBSON
MRS HEPWORTH
TIMOTHY WADLOW (TUBBY)
WILLIAM MOSSOP
JIM HEELER
ADA FIGGINS
FRED BEENSTOCK
DR MACFARLANE

The scene of the play is in Salford, Lancashire,
and the period is 1880.

ACT ONE   Interior of Hobson's Shop in Chapel Street
ACT TWO   The same
ACT THREE Will Mossop's shop in Oldfield Road
ACT FOUR   Living-room of Hobson's shop

Hobson's Choice was originally produced in America. The first London production took place on 22 June 1916 at the Apollo Theatre, with the following cast:

HENRY HORATIO HOBSON	Norman McKinnel
MAGGIE HOBSON	Edyth Goodall
WILLIAM MOSSOP	Joe Nightingale
ALICE HOBSON	Lydia Bilbrooke
VICKEY HOBSON	Hilda Davies
ALBERT PROSSER	Reginald Fry
FRED BEENSTOCK	Jefferson Gore
MRS HEPWORTH	Dora Gregory
TIMOTHY WADLOW	Sydney Paxton
JIM HEELER	J. Cooke Beresford
ADA FIGGINS	Mary Byron
DR MACFARLANE	J. Fisher White

The Play produced by NORMAN MCKINNEL

The play has had many notable productions since its first production in 1916, and it was included in the National Theatre repertory on 7 January 1964, with the following cast:

HENRY HORATIO HOBSON	Michael Redgrave
MAGGIE HOBSON	Joan Plowright
WILLIAM MOSSOP	Frank Finlay
ALICE HOBSON	Mary Miller
VICKEY HOBSON	Jeanne Hepple
ALBERT PROSSER	Terence Knapp
FRED BEENSTOCK	Raymond Clarke
MRS HEPWORTH	Enid Lorimer
TIMOTHY WADLOW	Reginald Green
JIM HEELER	Henry Lomax
ADA FIGGINS	Jean Rogers
DR MACFARLANE	Anthony Nichols

Scenery and costumes by MOTLEY
The Play directed by JOHN DEXTER

ACT ONE

The scene represents the interior of Hobson's Boot Shop in Chapel Street, Salford. The shop windows and entrance from street occupy the left side. Facing the audience is the counter, with exhibits of boots and slippers, behind which the wall is filled with racks containing boot boxes. Cane chairs in front of counter. There is a desk down left with a chair. A door right leads up to the house. In the centre of the stage is a trap leading to the cellar where work is done. There are no elaborate fittings. Gas brackets in the windows and walls. The business is prosperous, but to prosper in Salford in 1880 you did not require the elaborate accessories of a later day. A very important customer goes for fitting into Hobson's sitting-room. The rank and file use the cane chairs in the shop, which is dingy but business-like. The windows exhibit little stock, and amongst what there is clogs figure prominently. Through the windows comes the bright light of noon.

Sitting behind the counter are Hobson's two younger daughters, ALICE, *who is twenty-three, and* VICTORIA, *who is twenty-one, and very pretty.* ALICE *is knitting and* VICTORIA *is reading. They are in black, with neat black aprons. The door opens, and* MAGGIE *enters. She is Hobson's eldest daughter, thirty.*

ALICE: Oh, it's you. I hoped it was father going out.

MAGGIE: It isn't. (*She crosses and takes her place at desk.*)

ALICE: He *is* late this morning.

MAGGIE: He got up late. (*She busies herself with an account book.*)

VICKEY (*reading*): Has he had breakfast yet, Maggie?

MAGGIE: Breakfast! With a Masons' meeting last night?

VICKEY: He'll need reviving.

ALICE: Then I wish he'd go and do it.

VICKEY: Are you expecting anyone, Alice?

ALICE: Yes, I am, and you know I am, and I'll thank you both to go when he comes.

VICKEY: Well, I'll oblige you, Alice, if father's gone out first, only you know I can't leave the counter till he goes.

ALBERT PROSSER *enters from the street. He is twenty-six, nicely dressed, as the son of an established solicitor would be. He crosses to counter and raises his hat to Alice.*

ALBERT: Good morning, Miss Alice.

ALICE: Good morning, Mr Prosser. (*She leans across counter.*) Father's not gone out yet. He's late.

ALBERT: Oh! (*He turns to go, and is half-way to the door, when* MAGGIE *rises.*)

MAGGIE (*rising*): What can we do for you, Mr Prosser?

ALBERT (*stopping*): Well, I can't say that I came in to buy anything, Miss Hobson.

MAGGIE: This is a shop, you know. We're not here to let people go out without buying.

ALBERT: Well, I'll just have a pair of bootlaces, please.

MAGGIE: What size do you take in boots?

ALBERT: Eights. I've got small feet. (*He simpers, then perceives that Maggie is by no means smiling.*) Does that matter to the laces?

MAGGIE (*putting mat in front of armchair*): It matters to the boots. (*She pushes him slightly.*) Sit down, Mr Prosser.

ALBERT (*sitting*): Yes, but—

MAGGIE *is on her knees and takes off his boot.*

MAGGIE: It's time you had a new pair. These uppers are disgraceful for a professional man to wear. Number eights from the third rack, Vickey, please.

ALICE: Mr Prosser didn't come in to buy boots, Maggie.

VICKEY *comes down to Maggie with box, which she opens.*

MAGGIE: I wonder what does bring him in here so often?

ALBERT: I'm terrible hard on bootlaces, Miss Hobson.

    MAGGIE *puts a new boot on him and laces it.*

MAGGIE: Do you get through a pair a day? You must be strong.

ALBERT: I keep a little stock of them. It's as well to be prepared for accidents.

MAGGIE: And now you'll have boots to go with the laces, Mr Prosser. How does that feel?

ALBERT: Very comfortable.

MAGGIE: Try it standing up.

ALBERT (*trying and walking a few steps*): Yes, that fits all right.

MAGGIE: I'll put the other on.

ALBERT: Oh no, I really don't want to buy them.

MAGGIE (*pushing him*): Sit down, Mr Prosser. You can't go through the streets in odd boots.

ALBERT: What's the price of these?

MAGGIE: A pound.

ALBERT: A pound! I say—

MAGGIE: They're good boots, and you don't need to buy a pair of laces today, because we give them in as discount. Braid laces, that is. Of course, if you want leather ones, you being so strong in the arm and breaking so many pairs, you can have them, only it's tuppence more.

ALBERT: These – these will do.

MAGGIE: Very well, you'd better have the old pair mended and I'll send them home to you with the bill. (*She has laced the second boot, rises, and moves towards desk, throwing the boot box at* VICKEY, *who gives a little scream at the interruption of her reading.* ALBERT *gasps.*)

ALBERT: Well, if anyone had told me I was coming in here to spend a pound I'd have called him crazy.

MAGGIE: It's not wasted. Those boots will last. Good morning, Mr Prosser. (*She holds door open.*)

ALBERT: Good morning. (*He looks blankly at Alice and goes out*).

ALICE: Maggie, we know you're a pushing sales-woman, but—

MAGGIE (*returning to counter she picks up old boots and puts them on rack*): It'll teach him to keep out of here a bit. He's too much time on his hands.

ALICE: You know why he comes.

MAGGIE: I know it's time he paid a rent for coming. A pair of laces a day's not half enough. Coming here to make sheep's eyes at you. I'm sick of the sight of him.

ALICE: It's all very well for an old maid like you to talk, but if father won't have us go courting, where else can Albert meet me except here when father's out?

MAGGIE: If he wants to marry you why doesn't he do it?

ALICE: Courting must come first.

MAGGIE: It needn't. (*She picks up a slipper.*) See that slipper with a fancy buckle on to make it pretty? Courting's like that, my lass. All glitter and no use to nobody. (*She replaces slipper and sits at her desk.*)

   HENRY HORATIO HOBSON *enters from the house. He is fifty-five, successful, coarse, florid, and a parent of the period. His hat is on. It is one of those felt hats which are half-way to tall hats in shape. He has a heavy gold chain and masonic emblems on it. His clothes are bought to wear.*

HOBSON: Maggie, I'm just going out for a quarter of an hour.

MAGGIE: Yes, father. Don't be late for dinner. There's liver.

HOBSON: It's an hour off dinner-time. (*Going.*)

MAGGIE: So that, if you stay more than an hour in the Moon-raker's Inn, you'll be late for it.

HOBSON: 'Moonraker's'? Who said—? (*Turning.*)

VICKEY: If your dinner's ruined, it'll be your own fault.

HOBSON: Well, I'll be eternally—

ALICE: Don't swear, father.

HOBSON (*putting hat on counter*): No. I'll sit down instead. (*He takes a chair, straddling across it and facing them with his elbows on its back.*) Listen to me, you three. I've come to conclusions about you. And I won't have it. Do you hear that? Interfering

with my goings out and comings in. The idea! I've a mind
to take measures with the lot of you.

MAGGIE: I expect Mr Heeler's waiting for you in 'Moonraker's', father.

HOBSON: He can go on waiting. At present, I'm addressing a
few remarks to the rebellious females of this house, and what
I say will be listened to and heeded. I've noticed it coming on
ever since your mother died. There's been a gradual increase
of uppishness towards me.

VICKEY: Father, you'd have more time to talk after we've
closed tonight. (*She is anxious to resume her reading.*)

HOBSON: I'm talking now, and you're listening. Providence
has decreed that you should lack a mother's hand at the time
when single girls grow bumptious and must have somebody
to rule. But I'll tell you this, you'll none rule me.

VICKEY: I'm sure I'm not bumptious, father.

HOBSON: Yes, you are. You're pretty, but you're bumptious,
and I hate bumptiousness like I hate a lawyer.

ALICE: If we take trouble to feed you it's not bumptious to ask
you not to be late for your food.

VICKEY: Give and take, father.

HOBSON: I give and you take, and it's going to end.

MAGGIE: How much a week do you give us?

HOBSON: That's neither here nor there. (*Rises and moves to
doors.*) At moment I'm on uppishness, and I'm warning you
your conduct towards your parent's got to change. (*Turns
to the counter.*) But that's not all. That's private conduct, and
now I pass to broader aspects and I speak of public conduct.
I've looked upon my household as they go about the streets,
and I've been disgusted. The fair name and fame of Hobson
have been outraged by members of Hobson's family, and
uppishness has done it.

VICKEY: I don't know what you're talking about.

HOBSON: Vickey, you're pretty, but you can lie like a gas-
meter. Who had new dresses on last week?

ALICE: I suppose you mean Vickey and me?

HOBSON: I do.

VICKEY: We shall dress as we like, father, and you can save your breath.

HOBSON: I'm not stopping in from my business appointment for the purpose of saving my breath.

VICKEY: You like to see me in nice clothes.

HOBSON: I do. I like to see my daughters nice. That's why I pay Mr Tudsbury, the draper, £10 a year a head to dress you proper. It pleases the eye and it's good for trade. But, I'll tell you, if some women could see themselves as men see them, they'd have a shock, and I'll have words with Tudsbury an' all, for letting you dress up like guys. I saw you and Alice out of the 'Moonraker's' parlour on Thursday night and my friend Sam Minns—

ALICE: A publican.

HOBSON: Aye, a publican. As honest a man as God Almighty ever set behind a bar, my ladies. My friend, Sam Minns, asked me who you were. And well he might. You were going down Chapel Street with a hump added to nature behind you.

VICKEY (*scandalized*): Father!

HOBSON: The hump was wagging, and you put your feet on pavement as if you'd got chilblains – aye, stiff neck above and weak knees below. It's immodest!

ALICE: It is not immodest, father. It's the fashion to wear bustles.

HOBSON: Then to hell with the fashion.

MAGGIE: Father, you are not in the 'Moonraker's' now.

VICKEY: You should open your eyes to what other ladies wear. (*Rises.*)

HOBSON: If what I saw on you is any guide, I should do nowt of kind. I'm a decent-minded man. I'm Hobson. I'm British middle class and proud of it. I stand for common-sense and sincerity. You're affected, which is bad sense and insincerity.

You've overstepped nice dressing and you've tried grand
dressing – (VICKEY *sits*) – which is the occupation of fools
and such as have no brains. You forget the majesty of trade
and the unparalleled virtues of the British Constitution
which are all based on the sanity of the middle classes, com-
bined with the diligence of the working-classes. You're
losing balance, and you're putting the things which don't
matter in front of the things which do, and if you mean to
be a factor in the world in Lancashire or a factor in the house
of Hobson, you'll become sane.

VICKEY: Do you want us to dress like mill girls?

HOBSON: No. Nor like French Madams, neither. It's un-
English, I say.

ALICE: We shall continue to dress fashionably, father.

HOBSON: Then I've a choice for you two. Vickey, you I'm
talking to, and Alice. You'll become sane if you're going on
living here. You'll control this uppishness that's growing on
you. And if you don't, you'll get out of this, and exercise
your gifts on someone else than me. You don't know when
you're well off. But you'll learn it when I'm done with you.
I'll choose a pair of husbands for you, my girls. That's what
I'll do.

ALICE: Can't we choose husbands for ourselves?

HOBSON: I've been telling you for the last five minutes you're
not even fit to choose dresses for yourselves.

MAGGIE: You're talking a lot to Vickey and Alice, father.
Where do I come in?

HOBSON: You? (*Turning on her, astonished.*)

MAGGIE: If you're dealing husbands round, don't I get one?

HOBSON: Well, that's a good one! (*Laughs.*) You with a
husband!

MAGGIE: Why not?

HOBSON: Why not? I thought you'd sense enough to know.
But if you want the brutal truth, you're past the marrying
age. You're a proper old maid, Maggie, if ever there was one.

MAGGIE: I'm thirty.

HOBSON (*facing her*): Aye, thirty and shelved. Well, all the women can't get husbands. But you others, now. I've told you. I'll have less uppishness from you or else I'll shove you off my hands on to some other men. You can just choose which way you like. (*He picks up hat and makes for door.*)

MAGGIE: One o'clock dinner, father.

HOBSON: See here, Maggie. I set the hours at this house. It's one o'clock dinner because I say it is, and not because you do.

MAGGIE: Yes, father.

HOBSON: So long as that's clear I'll go. (*He is by door.*) Oh no, I won't. Mrs Hepworth's getting out of her carriage.

He puts hat on counter again. MAGGIE *rises and opens door. Enter* MRS HEPWORTH, *an old lady with a curt manner and good clothes.*

Good morning, Mrs Hepworth. What a lovely day! (*He places chair for her.*)

MRS HEPWORTH (*sitting*): Morning, Hobson. (*She raises her skirt.*) I've come about those boots you sent me home.

HOBSON (*kneeling and fondling her foot:*) Yes, Mrs Hepworth. They look very nice.

MRS HEPWORTH: Get up, Hobson. (*He scrambles up, controlling his feelings.*) You look ridiculous on the floor. Who made these boots?

HOBSON: We did. Our own make.

MRS HEPWORTH: Will you answer a plain question? Who made these boots?

HOBSON: They were made on the premises.

MRS HEPWORTH (*to Maggie*): Young woman, you seemed to have some sense when you served me. Can you answer me?

MAGGIE: I think so, but I'll make sure for you, Mrs Hepworth. (*She opens trap and calls.*) Tubby!

HOBSON: You wish to see the identical workman, madam?

MRS HEPWORTH: I said so.

HOBSON: I am responsible for all work turned out here.

MRS HEPWORTH: I never said you weren't.

> TUBBY WADLOW *comes up trap. A white-haired little man with thin legs and a paunch, in dingy clothes with no collar and a coloured cotton shirt. He has no coat on.*

TUBBY: Yes, Miss Maggie? (*He stands half out of trap, not coming right up.*)

MRS HEPWORTH: Man, did you make these boots? (*She rises and advances one pace towards him.*)

TUBBY: No, ma'am.

MRS HEPWORTH: Then who did? Am I to question every soul in the place before I find out?

TUBBY: They're Willie's making, those.

MRS HEPWORTH: Then tell Willie I want him.

TUBBY: Certainly, ma'am. (*He goes down trap and calls*) Willie!

MRS HEPWORTH: Who's Willie?

HOBSON: Name of Mossop, madam. But if there is anything wrong I assure you I'm capable of making the man suffer for it. I'll—

> WILLIE MOSSOP *comes up trap. He is a lanky fellow, about thirty, not naturally stupid but stunted mentally by a brutalized childhood. He is a raw material of a charming man, but, at present, it requires a very keen eye to detect his potentialities. His clothes are an even poorer edition of Tubby's. He comes half-way up trap.*

MRS HEPWORTH: Are you Mossop?

WILLIE: Yes, mum.

MRS HEPWORTH: You made these boots?

WILLIE (*peering at them*): Yes, I made them last week.

MRS HEPWORTH: Take that.

> WILLIE, *bending down, rather expects 'that' to be a blow. Then he raises his head and finds she is holding out a visiting card. He takes it.*

See what's on it?

WILLIE (*bending over the card*): Writing?

MRS HEPWORTH: Read it.

WILLIE: I'm trying. (*His lips move as he tries to spell it out.*)

MRS HEPWORTH: Bless the man. Can't you read?

WILLIE: I do a bit. Only it's such a funny print.

MRS HEPWORTH: It's the usual italics of a visiting card, my man. Now listen to me. I heard about this shop, and what I heard brought me here for these boots. I'm particular about what I put on my feet.

HOBSON: I assure you it shall not occur again, Mrs Hepworth.

MRS HEPWORTH: What shan't?

HOBSON (*crestfallen*): I – I don't know.

MRS HEPWORTH: Then hold your tongue. Mossop, I've tried every shop in Manchester, and these are the best-made pair of boots I've ever had. Now, you'll make my boots in future. You hear that, Hobson?

HOBSON: Yes, madam, of course he shall.

MRS HEPWORTH: You'll keep that card, Mossop, and you won't dare leave here to go to another shop without letting me know where you are.

HOBSON: Oh, he won't make a change.

MRS HEPWORTH: How do you know? The man's a treasure, and I expect you underpay him.

HOBSON: That'll do, Willie. You can go.

WILLIE: Yes, sir.

He dives down trap. MAGGIE *closes it.*

MRS HEPWORTH: He's like a rabbit.

MAGGIE: Can I take your order for another pair of boots, Mrs Hepworth?

MRS HEPWORTH: Not yet, young woman. But I shall send my daughters here. And, mind you, that man's to make the boots.

MAGGIE: Certainly, Mrs Hepworth.

HOBSON *opens door.*

MRS HEPWORTH: Good morning.

HOBSON: Good morning, Mrs Hepworth. Very glad to have the honour of serving you, madam.

She goes out. HOBSON *closes door.*

I wish some people would mind their own business. What does she want to praise a workman to his face for?

MAGGIE: I suppose he deserved it.

HOBSON: Deserved be blowed! Making them uppish. That's what it is. Last time she puts her foot in my shop, I give you my word.

MAGGIE: Don't be silly, father.

HOBSON: I'll show her. Thinks she owns the earth because she lives at Hope Hall.

Enter from street JIM HEELER, *who is a grocer, and Hobson's boon companion.*

JIM: (*looking down street as he enters*): That's a bit of a startler.

HOBSON (*swinging round*): Eh? Oh, morning, Jim.

JIM: You're doing a good class trade if the carriage folk come to you, Hobson.

HOBSON: What?

JIM: Wasn't that Mrs Hepworth?

HOBSON: Oh yes. Mrs Hepworth's an old and valued customer of mine.

JIM: It's funny you deal with Hope Hall and never mentioned it.

HOBSON: Why, I've made boots for her and all her circle for . . . how long, Maggie? Oh, I dunno.

JIM: You kept it dark. Well, aren't you coming round yonder?

HOBSON (*reaching for his hat*): Yes. That is, no.

JIM: Are you ill?

HOBSON: No. Get away, you girls. I'll look after the shop. I want to talk to Mr Heeler.

JIM: Well, can't you talk in the 'Moonraker's'?

The girls go out to house, MAGGIE *last.*

HOBSON: Yes, with Sam Minns, and Denton and Tudsbury there.

JIM: It's private, then. What's the trouble, Henry?

HOBSON *waves* JIM *into chair and sits.*

HOBSON: They're the trouble. (*Indicates door to house.*) Do your daughters worry you, Jim?

JIM: Nay, they mostly do as I bid them, and the missus does the leathering if they don't.

HOBSON: Ah, Jim, a wife's a handy thing, and you don't know it proper till she's taken from you. I felt grateful for the quiet when my Mary fell on rest, but I can see my mistake now. I used to think I was hard put to it to fend her off when she wanted summat out of me, but the dominion of one woman is Paradise to the dominion of three.

JIM: It sounds a sad case, Henry.

HOBSON: I'm a talkative man by nature, Jim. You know that.

JIM: You're an orator, Henry. I doubt John Bright himself is better gifted of the gab than you.

HOBSON: Nay, that's putting it a bit too strong. A good case needs no flattery.

JIM: Well, you're the best debater in the 'Moonraker's' parlour.

HOBSON: And that's no more than truth. Yes, Jim, in the estimation of my fellow men, I give forth words of weight. In the eyes of my daughters I'm a windbag.

JIM: Nay. Never!

HOBSON: I am. They scorn my wisdom, Jim. They answer back. I'm landed in a hole – a great and undignified hole. My own daughters have got the upper hand of me.

JIM: Women are worse than men for getting above themselves.

HOBSON: A woman's foolishness begins where man's leaves off.

JIM: They want a firm hand, Henry.

HOBSON: I've lifted up my voice and roared at them.

JIM: Beware at roaring at women, Henry. Roaring is mainly hollow sound. It's like trying to defeat an army with banging drums instead of cold steel. And it's steel in a man's character that subdues the women.

HOBSON: I've tried all ways, and I'm fair moithered. I dunno what to do.

JIM: Then you quit roaring at 'em and get 'em wed.

HOBSON: I've thought of that. Trouble is to find the men.

JIM: Men's common enough. Are you looking for angels in breeches?

HOBSON: I'd like my daughters to wed temperance young men, Jim.

JIM: You keep your ambitions within reasonable limits, Henry. You've three daughters to find husbands for.

HOBSON: Two, Jim, two.

JIM: Two?

HOBSON: Vickey and Alice are mostly window dressing in shop. But Maggie's too useful to part with. And she's a bit on the ripe side for marrying, is our Maggie.

JIM: I've seen 'em do it at double her age. Still, leaving her out, you've two.

HOBSON: One'll do for a start, Jim. It's a thing I've noticed about wenches. Get one wedding in a family and it goes through the lot like measles.

JIM: Well, you want a man, and you want him temperance. It'll cost you a bit, you know.

HOBSON: Eh? Oh, I'll get my hand down for the wedding all right.

JIM: A warm man like you 'ull have to do more than that. There's things called settlements.

HOBSON: Settlements?

JIM: Aye. You've to bait your hook to catch fish, Henry.

HOBSON: Then I'll none go fishing.

JIM: But you said—

HOBSON: I've changed my mind. I'd a fancy for a bit of peace, but there's luxuries a man can buy too dear. Settlements indeed!

JIM: I had a man in mind.

HOBSON: You keep him there, Jim. I'll rub along and chance it. Settlements indeed!

JIM: You save their keep.

HOBSON: They work for that. And they're none of them big eaters.

JIM: And their wages.

HOBSON: Wages? Do you think I pay wages to my own daughters? I'm not a fool.

JIM: Then it's all off?

HOBSON: From the moment that you breathed the word 'settlements' it was dead off, Jim. Let's go to the 'Moonraker's' and forget there's such a thing as women in the world. (*He takes up hat and rings bell on counter.*) Shop! Shop!

   MAGGIE *enters.*

I'm going out, Maggie.

MAGGIE (*she remains by door*): Dinner's at one, remember.

HOBSON: Dinner will be when I come in for it. I'm master here.

MAGGIE: Yes, father. One o'clock.

HOBSON: Come along, Jim.

   JIM *and* HOBSON *go out to street.* MAGGIE *turns to speak inside house door.*

MAGGIE: Dinner at half-past one, girls. We'll give him half an hour. (*She closes door and moves to trap, which she raises.*) Willie, come here.

   In a moment WILLIE *appears, and stops half-way up.*

WILLIE: Yes, Miss Maggie?

MAGGIE: Come up, and put the trap down; I want to talk to you.

   He comes, reluctantly.

WILLIE: We're very busy in the cellar.

   MAGGIE *points to trap. He closes it.*

MAGGIE: Show me your hands, Willie.

WILLIE: They're dirty. (*He holds them out hesitatingly.*)

MAGGIE: Yes, they're dirty, but they're clever. They can shape the leather like no other man's that ever came into the shop. Who taught you, Willie? (*She retains his hands.*)

WILLIE: Why, Miss Maggie, I learnt my trade here.

MAGGIE: Hobson's never taught you to make boots the way you do.

WILLIE: I've had no other teacher.

MAGGIE (*dropping his hands*): And needed none. You're a natural born genius at making boots. It's a pity you're a natural fool at all else.

WILLIE: I'm not much good at owt but leather, and that's a fact.

MAGGIE: When are you going to leave Hobson's?

WILLIE: Leave Hobson's? I – I thought I gave satisfaction.

MAGGIE: Don't you want to leave?

WILLIE: Not me. I've been at Hobson's all my life, and I'm not leaving till I'm made.

MAGGIE: I said you were a fool.

WILLIE: Then I'm a loyal fool.

MAGGIE: Don't you want to get on, Will Mossop? You heard what Mrs Hepworth said. You know the wages you get and you know the wages a bootmaker like you could get in one of the big shops in Manchester.

WILLIE: Nay, I'd be feared to go in them fine places.

MAGGIE: What keeps you here? Is it the – the people?

WILLIE: I dunno what it is. I'm used to being here.

MAGGIE: Do you know what keeps this business on its legs? Two things: one's the good boots you make that sell themselves, the other's the bad boots other people make and I sell. We're a pair, Will Mossop.

WILLIE: You're a wonder in the shop, Miss Maggie.

MAGGIE: And you're a marvel in the workshop. Well?

WILLIE: Well, what?

MAGGIE: It seems to me to point one way.

WILLIE: What way is that?

MAGGIE: You're leaving me to do the work, my lad.

WILLIE: I'll be getting back to my stool, Miss Maggie. (*Moves to trap.*)

MAGGIE (*stopping him*): You'll go back when I've done with

you. I've watched you for a long time and everything I've seen, I've liked. I think you'll do for me.

WILLIE: What way, Miss Maggie?

MAGGIE: Will Mossop, you're my man. Six months I've counted on you and it's got to come out some time.

WILLIE: But I never—

MAGGIE: I know you never, or it 'ud not be left to me to do the job like this.

WILLIE: I'll – I'll sit down. (*He sits in arm-chair, mopping his brow.*) I'm feeling queer-like. What dost want me for?

MAGGIE: To invest in. You're a business idea in the shape of a man.

WILLIE: I've got no head for business at all.

MAGGIE: But I have. My brain and your hands 'ull make a working partnership.

WILLIE (*getting up, relieved*): Partnership! Oh, that's a different thing. I thought you were axing me to wed you.

MAGGIE: I am.

WILLIE: Well, by gum! And you the master's daughter.

MAGGIE: Maybe that's why, Will Mossop. Maybe I've had enough of father, and you're as different from him as any man I know.

WILLIE: It's a bit awkward-like.

MAGGIE: And you don't help me any, lad. What's awkward about it?

WILLIE: You talking to me like this.

MAGGIE: I'll tell you something, Will. It's a poor sort of woman who'll stay lazy when she sees her best chance slipping from her. A Salford life's too near the bone to lose things through fear of speaking out.

WILLIE: I'm your best chance?

MAGGIE: You are that, Will.

WILLIE: Well, by gum! I never thought of this.

MAGGIE: Think of it now.

WILLIE: I am doing. Only the blow's a bit too sudden to think very clear. I've a great respect for you, Miss Maggie. You're a shapely body, and you're a masterpiece at selling in the shop, but when it comes to marrying, I'm bound to tell you that I'm none in love with you.

MAGGIE: Wait till you're asked. I want your hand in mine and your word for it that you'll go through life with me for the best we can get out of it.

WILLIE: We'd not get much without there's love between us, lass.

MAGGIE: I've got the love all right.

WILLIE: Well, I've not, and that's honest.

MAGGIE: We'll get along without.

WILLIE: You're desperate set on this. It's a puzzle to me all ways. What 'ud your father say?

MAGGIE: He'll say a lot, and he can say it. It'll make no difference to me.

WILLIE: Much better not upset him. It's not worth while.

MAGGIE: I'm judge of that. You're going to wed me, Will.

WILLIE: Oh, nay, I'm not. Really I can't do that, Maggie. I can see that I'm disturbing your arrangements like, but I'll be obliged if you'll put this notion from you.

MAGGIE: When I make arrangements, my lad, they're not made for upsetting.

WILLIE: What makes it so desperate awkward is that I'm tokened.

MAGGIE: You're what?

WILLIE: I'm tokened to Ada Figgins.

MAGGIE: Then you'll get loose and quick. Who's Ada Figgins? Do I know her?

WILLIE: I'm the lodger at her mother's.

MAGGIE: The scheming hussy. It's not that sandy girl who brings your dinner?

WILLIE: She's golden-haired is Ada. Aye, she'll be here soon.

MAGGIE: And so shall I. I'll talk to Ada. I've seen her and I know the breed. Ada's the helpless sort.

WILLIE: She needs protecting.

MAGGIE: That's how she got you, was it? Yes, I can see her clinging round your neck, until you fancied you were strong. But I'll tell you this, my lad, it's a desperate poor kind of a woman that'll look for protection to the likes of you.

WILLIE: Ada does.

MAGGIE: And that gives me the weight of her. She's born to meekness, Ada is. You wed her, and you'll be an eighteen shilling a week bootmaker all the days of your life. You'll be a slave, and a contented slave.

WILLIE: I'm not ambitious that I know of.

MAGGIE: No. But you're going to be. I'll see to that. I've got my work cut out, but there's the makings of a man about you.

WILLIE: I wish you'd leave me alone.

MAGGIE: So does the fly when the spider catches him. You're my man, Willie Mossop.

WILLIE: Aye, so you say. Ada would tell another story, though.

ADA FIGGINS *enters from the street. She is not ridiculous, but a weak, poor-blooded, poor-spirited girl of twenty, in clogs and shawl, with Willie's dinner in a basin carried in a blue handkerchief. She crosses to him and gives him the basin.*

ADA: There's your dinner, Will.

WILLIE: Thank you, Ada.

She turns to go, and finds Maggie in her way.

MAGGIE: I want a word with you. You're treading on my foot, young woman.

ADA: Me, Miss Hobson? (*She looks stupidly at Maggie's feet.*)

MAGGIE: What's this with you and him?

ADA (*gushing*): Oh, Miss 'Obson, it is good of you to take notice like that.

WILLIE: Ada, she—

MAGGIE: You hold your hush. This is for me and her to settle. Take a fair look at him, Ada.

ADA: At Will?

MAGGIE (*nodding*): Not much for two women to fall out over, is there?

ADA: Maybe he's not so much to look at, but you should hear him play.

MAGGIE: Play? Are you a musician, Will?

WILLIE: I play the Jew's harp.

MAGGIE: That's what you see in him, is it? A gawky fellow that plays the Jew's harp?

ADA: I see the lad I love, Miss 'Obson.

MAGGIE: It's a funny thing, but I can say the same.

ADA: You!

WILLIE: That's what I've been trying to tell you, Ada, and – and, by gum, she'll have me from you if you don't be careful.

MAGGIE: So we're quits so far, Ada.

ADA: You'll pardon me. You've spoke too late. Will and me's tokened.

MAGGIE: That's the past. It's the future that I'm looking to. What's your idea for that?

ADA: You mind your own business, Miss 'Obson. Will Mossop's no concern of thine.

WILLIE: That's what I try to tell her myself, only she will have it it's no use.

MAGGIE: Not an atom. I've asked for your idea of Willie's future. If it's a likelier one than mine, I'll give you best and you can have the lad.

ADA: I'm trusting him to make the future right.

MAGGIE: It's as bad as I thought it was. Willie, you wed me.

ADA (*weakly*): It's daylight robbery.

WILLIE: Aren't you going to put up a better fight for me than that, Ada? You're fair giving me to her.

MAGGIE: Will Mossop, you take orders from me in this shop. I've told you you'll wed me.

WILLIE: Seems like there's no escape.

ADA: Wait while I get you to home, my lad. I'll set my mother on to you.

MAGGIE: Oh, so it's her mother made this match?

WILLIE: She had above a bit to do with it.

MAGGIE: I've got no mother, Will.

WILLIE: You need none, neither.

MAGGIE: Well, can I sell you a pair of clogs, Miss Figgins?

ADA: No. Nor anything else.

MAGGIE: Then you've no business here, have you? (*Moves up to doors and opens them.*)

ADA (*going to him*): Will, are you going to see me ordered out?

WILLIE: It's her shop, Ada.

ADA: You mean I'm to go like this?

WILLIE: She means it.

ADA: It's cruel hard. (*Moves towards doors.*)

MAGGIE: When it comes to a parting, it's best to part sudden and no whimpering about it.

ADA: I'm not whimpering, and I'm not parting, neither. But he'll whimper tonight when my mother sets about him.

MAGGIE: That'll do.

ADA: Will Mossop, I'm telling you, you'll come home tonight to a thick ear. (*She goes.*)

WILLIE: I'd really rather wed Ada, Maggie, if it's all same to you.

MAGGIE: Why? Because of her mother?

WILLIE: She's a terrible rough side to her tongue, has Mrs Figgins.

MAGGIE: Are you afraid of her?

WILLIE (*hesitates, then says*): Yes.

MAGGIE: You needn't be.

WILLIE: Yes, but you don't know her. She'll jaw me till I'm black in the face when I go home tonight.

MAGGIE: You won't go home tonight.

WILLIE: Not go!

MAGGIE: You've done with lodging there. You'll go to Tubby

Wadlow's when you knock off work and Tubby 'ull go round to Mrs Figgins for your things.

WILLIE: And I'm not to go back there never no more?

MAGGIE: No.

WILLIE: It's like an 'appy dream. Eh, Maggie, you do manage things.

He opens the trap.

MAGGIE: And while Tubby's there you can go round and see about putting the banns up for us two.

WILLIE: Banns! Oh, but I'm hardly used to the idea yet.

MAGGIE: You'll have three weeks to get used to it in. Now you can kiss me, Will.

WILLIE: That's forcing things a bit, and all. It's like saying I agree to everything, a kiss is.

MAGGIE: Yes.

WILLIE: And I don't agree yet. I'm—

MAGGIE: Come along.

ALICE, *then* VICKEY *enter from house.*

Do what I tell you, Will.

WILLIE: Now? With them here?

MAGGIE: Yes.

WILLIE (*pause*): I couldn't. (*He dives for trap, runs down, and closes it.*)

ALICE: What's the matter with Willie?

MAGGIE: He's a bit upset because I've told him he's to marry me. Is dinner cooking nicely?

ALICE: You're going to marry Willie Mossop! Willie Mossop!

VICKEY: You've kept it quiet, Maggie.

MAGGIE: You know about it pretty near as soon as Willie does himself.

VICKEY: Well, I don't know!

ALICE: I know, and if you're afraid to speak your thoughts, I'm not. Look here, Maggie, what you do touches us, and you're mistaken if you think I'll own Willie Mossop for my brother-in-law.

MAGGIE: Is there supposed to be some disgrace in him?

ALICE: You ask father if there's disgrace. And look at me. I'd hopes of Albert Prosser till this happened.

MAGGIE: You'll marry Albert Prosser when he's able, and that'll be when he starts spending less on laundry bills and hair cream.

HOBSON *enters from the street.*

HOBSON: Well, what about that dinner?

MAGGIE: It'll be ready in ten minutes.

HOBSON: You said one o'clock.

MAGGIE: Yes, father. One for half-past. If you'll wash your hands it'll be ready as soon as you are.

HOBSON: I won't wash my hands. I don't hold with such finicking ways, and well you know it.

VICKEY: Father, have you heard the news about our Maggie?

HOBSON: News? There is no news. It's the same old tale. Uppishness. You'd keep a starving man from the meat he earns in the sweat of his brow, would you? I'll put you in your places. I'll—

MAGGIE: Don't lose your temper, father. You'll maybe need it soon when Vickey speaks.

HOBSON: What's Vickey been doing?

VICKEY: Nothing. It's about Will Mossop, father.

HOBSON: Will?

ALICE: Yes. What's your opinion of Will?

HOBSON: A decent lad. I've nowt against him that I know of.

ALICE: Would you like him in the family?

HOBSON: Whose family?

VICKEY: Yours.

MAGGIE: I'm going to marry Willie, father. That's what all the fuss is about.

HOBSON: Marry – you – Mossop!

MAGGIE: You thought me past the marrying age. I'm not. That's all.

HOBSON: Didn't you hear me say I'd do the choosing when it came to a question of husbands?

MAGGIE: You said I was too old to get a husband.

HOBSON: You are. You all are.

VICKEY: Father!

HOBSON: And if you're not, it makes no matter. I'll have no husbands here.

ALICE: But you said—

HOBSON: I've changed my mind. I've learnt some things since then. There's a lot too much expected of a father nowadays. There'll be no weddings here.

ALICE: Oh, father!

HOBSON: Go and get my dinner served and talk less. Go on now. I'm not in right temper to be crossed.

He drives Alice and Vickey before him. They go out protesting loudly. But MAGGIE *stands in his way as he follows and she closes the door. She looks at him from the stair.*

MAGGIE: You and I 'ull be straight with one another, father. I'm not a fool and you're not a fool, and things may as well be put in their places as left untidy.

HOBSON: I tell you my mind's made up. You can't have Willie Mossop. Why, lass, his father was a workhouse brat. A come-by-chance.

MAGGIE: It's news to me we're snobs in Salford. I'll have Willie Mossop. I've to settle my life's course, and a good course, too, so think on.

HOBSON: I'd be the laughing-stock of the place if I allowed it. I won't have it, Maggie. It's hardly decent at your time of life.

MAGGIE: I'm thirty and I'm marrying Willie Mossop. And now I'll tell you my terms.

HOBSON: You're in a nice position to state terms, my lass.

MAGGIE: You will pay my man, Will Mossop, the same wages as before. And as for me, I've given you the better part of twenty years of work without wages. I'll work eight hours a day in future and you will pay me fifteen shillings by the week.

HOBSON: Do you think I'm made of brass?

MAGGIE: You'll soon be made of less than you are if you let Willie go. And if Willie goes, I go. That's what you've got to face.

HOBSON: I might face it, Maggie. Shop hands are cheap.

MAGGIE: Cheap ones are cheap. The sort you'd have to watch all day, and you'd feel happy helping them to tie up parcels and sell laces with Tudsbury and Heeler and Minns supping their ale without you. I'm value to you, so's my man; and you can boast it at the 'Moonraker's' that your daughter Maggie's made the strangest, finest match a woman's made this fifty year. And you can put your hand in your pocket and do what I propose.

HOBSON: I'll show you what I propose, Maggie. (*He lifts trap and calls.*) Will Mossop! (*He places hat on counter and unbuckles belt.*) I cannot leather you, my lass. You're female, and exempt, but I can leather him. Come up, Will Mossop.

WILL *comes up trap and closes it.*

You've taken up with my Maggie, I hear. (*He conceals strap.*)

WILLIE: Nay, I've not. She's done the taking up.

HOBSON: Well, Willie, either way, you've fallen on misfortune. Love's led you astray, and I feel bound to put you right. (*Shows strap.*)

WILLIE: Maggie, what's this?

MAGGIE: I'm watching you, my lad.

HOBSON: Mind, Willie, you can keep your job. I don't bear malice, but we must beat the love from your body, and every morning you come here to work with love still sitting in you, you'll get a leathering. (*Getting ready to strike.*)

WILLIE: You'll not beat love in me. You're making a great mistake, Mr Hobson, and—

HOBSON: You'll put aside your weakness for my Maggie if you've a liking for a sound skin. You'll waste a gradely lot of brass at chemist's if I am at you for a week with this. (*He swings the strap.*)

WILLIE: I'm none wanting thy Maggie, it's her that's after me, but I'll tell you this, Mr Hobson: if you touch me with that belt, I'll take her quick, aye, and stick to her like glue.

HOBSON: There's nobbut one answer to that kind of talk, my lad. (*He strikes with belt.* MAGGIE *shrinks.*)

WILLIE: And I've nobbut one answer back. Maggie, I've none kissed you yet. I shirked before. But, by gum, I'll kiss you now – (*he kisses her quickly, with temper, not with passion, as quickly leaves her, to face Hobson*) – and take you and hold you. And if Mr Hobson raises up that strap again, I'll do more. I'll walk straight out of shop with thee and us two 'ull set up for ourselves.

MAGGIE: Willie! I knew you had it in you, lad. (*She puts her arm round his neck. He is quite unresponsive. His hands fall limply to his sides.*)

HOBSON *stands in amazed indecision.*

CURTAIN

ACT TWO

A month later. The shop as Act One. It is about mid-day. ALICE *is in Maggie's chair at the desk, some ledgers in front of her, and* VICKEY *is reading behind the counter. The trap is open and* TUBBY *stands near the desk by Alice.*

ALICE: I'm sure I don't know what to tell you to do, Tubby.

TUBBY: There's nothing in at all to start on, Miss Alice. We're worked up.

ALICE: Well, father's out and I can't help you.

TUBBY: He'll play old Harry if he comes in and finds us doing nowt in the workroom.

VICKEY: Then do something. We're not stopping you.

TUBBY: You're not telling me neither. And I'm supposed to take my orders from the shop.

ALICE: I don't know what to tell you. Nobody seems to want any boots made.

TUBBY: The high-class trade has dropped like a stone this last month. Of course we can go on making clogs for stock if you like.

ALICE: Then you'd better.

TUBBY: You know what's got by selling clogs won't pay the rent, let alone wages, but if clogs are your orders, Miss Alice— (*He moves towards trap.*)

ALICE: You suggested it.

TUBBY: I made the remark. (*Starts going down.*) But I'm not a rash man, and I'm not going to be responsible to the master with his temper so nowty and all since Miss Maggie went.

26

ALICE: Oh, dear! What would Miss Maggie have told you to do?

TUBBY: I couldn't tell you that, Miss, I'm sure. I don't recollect things being as slack as this in her time.

VICKEY: You don't help us much for an intelligent fore-man.

TUBBY: When you've told me what to do, I'll use my in-telligence and see it's done properly.

ALICE: Then go and make clogs.

TUBBY: Them's your orders?

ALICE: Yes.

TUBBY: Thank you, Miss Alice.

    TUBBY *goes down trap and closes it.*

ALICE: I wonder if I've done right?

VICKEY: That's your look-out.

ALICE: I don't care. It's father's place to be here to tell them what to do.

VICKEY: Maggie used to manage without him.

ALICE: Oh, yes. Go on. Blame me that the place is all at sixes and sevens.

VICKEY: I don't blame you. I know as well as you do that it's father's fault. He ought to look after his business himself instead of wasting more time than ever in the 'Moonraker's', but you needn't be snappy with me about it.

ALICE: I'm not snappy in myself. (*Sitting at desk.*) It's these figures. I can't get them right. What's 17 and 25?

VICKEY (*promptly*): Fifty-two, of course.

ALICE: Well, it doesn't balance right. Oh, I wish I was married and out of it.

VICKEY: Same here.

ALICE: You!

VICKEY: You needn't think you're the only one.

ALICE: Well, you're sly, Vickey Hobson. You've kept it to yourself.

VICKEY: It's just as well now that I did. Maggie's spoilt our chances for ever. Nobody's fretting to get Willie Mossop for a brother-in-law.

MAGGIE *enters, followed by* FREDDY BEENSTOCK *and then* WILL. *Maggie and Will are actually about to be married, but their dress does not specially indicate it. They are not in their older clothes, and that is all.* FREDDY *is smarter than either, though only in his everyday dress. He is not at all a blood, but the respectable son of a respectable tradesman, and his appearance is such as to justify his attractiveness in Vickey's eyes.*

ALICE: Maggie, you here!

MAGGIE: I thought we'd just drop in. Vickey, what's this that Mr Beenstock's telling me about you and him?

VICKEY (*sullenly*): If he's told you, I suppose you know.

FREDDY (*smilingly*): She got it out of me, Vickey.

VICKEY: I don't know that it's any business of yours, Maggie.

MAGGIE: You'll never get no farther with it by yourselves from what I hear of father's carryings-on.

VICKEY: That's your fault. Yours and his. (*Indicating* WILLIE *who is trying to efface himself at the back.*)

MAGGIE (*sharply*): Leave that alone. I'm here to help you if you'll have my help.

VICKEY *would say 'No' but—*

FREDDY: It's very good of you, Miss Maggie, I must say. Your father has turned very awkward.

MAGGIE: I reckon he'll change. Has your young man been in yet this morning, Alice?

ALICE (*indignantly*): My young—

MAGGIE: Albert Prosser.

ALICE: No.

MAGGIE: Do you expect him?

ALICE: He's not been here so often since you and Willie Mossop got—

MAGGIE (*sharply*): Since when?

ALICE: Since you made him buy that pair of boots he didn't want.

MAGGIE: I see. He didn't like paying for taking his pleasure in our shop. Well, if he's not expected, somebody must go for him. Prosser, Pilkington & Prosser, Solicitors of Bexley Square. That's right, isn't it?

ALICE: Yes. Albert's 'and Prosser'.

MAGGIE: Aye? Quite a big man in his way. Then, will you go and fetch him, Mr Beenstock? Tell him to bring the paper with him.

VICKEY (*indignantly*): *You*'re ordering folk about a bit.

MAGGIE: I'm used to it.

FREDDY: It's all right, Vickey.

ALICE: Is it? Suppose father comes in and finds Albert and Freddy here?

MAGGIE: He won't.

ALICE: He's beyond his time already.

MAGGIE: I know. You must have worried father very badly since I went, Alice.

ALICE: Why?

MAGGIE: Tell them, Mr Beenstock.

FREDDY: Well, the fact is, Mr Hobson won't come because he's at our place just now.

VICKEY: At your corn warehouse? What's father doing there?

FREDDY: He's – he's sleeping, Vickey.

ALICE: Sleeping?

FREDDY: You see, we've a cellar trap in our place that opens in the pavement and your father – wasn't looking very carefully where he was going and he fell into it.

VICKEY: Fell? Is father hurt?

FREDDY: He's snoring very loudly, but he isn't hurt. He fell soft on some bags.

MAGGIE: Now you can go for Albert Prosser.

ALICE: Is that all we're to be told?

MAGGIE: It's all there is to tell till Freddy's seen his solicitor.

FREDDY (*to Vickey*): I'll not be long.

MAGGIE: Don't. I've a job here for you when you get back.

FREDDY *goes out.*

ALICE: I don't know what you're aiming at, Maggie, but—

MAGGIE: The difference between us is that I do. I always did.

VICKEY (*indicating Willie*): It's a queer thing you aimed at.

MAGGIE (*taking Will's arm*): I've done uncommon well myself, and I've come here to put things straight for you. Father told you to get married and you don't shape.

ALICE: He changed his mind.

MAGGIE: I don't allow for folks to change their minds. He made his choice. He said get married, and you're going to.

VICKEY: You haven't made it easier for us, you know.

MAGGIE: Meaning Willie?

WILLIE: It wasn't my fault, Miss Vickey, really it wasn't.

MAGGIE: You call her Vickey, Will.

VICKEY: No, he doesn't.

MAGGIE: He's in the family or going to be. And I'll tell you this. If you want your Freddy, and if you want your Albert, you'll be respectful to my Willie.

ALICE: Willie Mossop was our boot hand.

MAGGIE: He was, and you'll let bygones be bygones. He's as good as you are now, and better.

WILLIE: Nay, come, Maggie—

MAGGIE: Better, I say. They're shop assistants. You're your own master, aren't you?

WILLIE: I've got my name wrote up on the windows, but I dunno so much about being master.

MAGGIE (*producing card*): That's his business card: William Mossop, Practical Boot and Shoe Maker, 39a Oldfield Road, Salford. William Mossop, Master Bootmaker! That's the man you're privileged to call by his Christian name. Aye, and I'll do more for you than let you call him in his name. You can both of you kiss him for your brother-in-law to be.

WILLIE: Nay, Maggie, I'm no great hand at kissing.

VICKEY *and* ALICE *are much annoyed.*

MAGGIE (*dryly*): I've noticed that. A bit of practice will do you no harm. Come along, Vickey.

ALICE (*interposing*): But, Maggie . . . a shop of your own—

MAGGIE (*grimly*): I'm waiting, Vickey.

WILLIE: I don't see that you ought to drive her to it, Maggie.

MAGGIE: You hold your hush.

ALICE: But however did you manage it? Where did the capital come from?

MAGGIE: It came. Will, stand still. She's making up her mind to it.

WILLIE: I'd just as lief not put her to the trouble.

MAGGIE: You'll take your proper place in this family, my lad, trouble or no trouble.

VICKEY: I don't see why you should always get your way.

MAGGIE: It's just a habit. Come along now, Vickey, I've a lot to do today and you're holding everything back.

VICKEY: It's under protest.

MAGGIE: Protest, but kiss.

VICKEY *kisses* WILL, *who finds he rather likes it. She moves back and starts dusting furiously.*

Your turn now, Alice.

ALICE: I'll do it if you'll help me with these books, Maggie.

MAGGIE: Books? Father's put you in my place?

ALICE: Yes.

MAGGIE: Then he must take the consequences. Your books aren't my affair.

ALICE: I think you might help me, Maggie.

MAGGIE: I'm surprised at you, Alice, I really am, after what you've just been told. Exposing your books to a rival shop. You ought to know better. Will's waiting. And you're to kiss him hearty now.

ALICE: Very well. (*She kisses Will.*)

WILLIE: There's more in kissing nice young women than I thought.

MAGGIE: Don't get too fond of it, my lad.

ALICE: Well, I hope you're satisfied, Maggie. You've got your way again, and now perhaps you'll tell us if there's anything you want in this shop.

MAGGIE: Eh? Are you trying to sell me something?

ALICE: I'm asking you, what's your business here?

MAGGIE: I've told you once. Will and me's taking a day off to put you in the way of getting wed.

VICKEY: It looks like things are slow at your new shop if you can walk round in your best clothes on a working day.

WILLIE: It's not a working day with us. It's a wedding-day.

ALICE: You've been married this morning!

MAGGIE: Not us. I'll have my sisters there when I get wed. It's at one o'clock at St Philip's.

VICKEY: But we can't leave the shop to come.

MAGGIE: Why not? Is trade so brisk?

VICKEY: No, but—

MAGGIE: Not so much high-class trade doing with you, eh?

ALICE: I don't see how you knew.

MAGGIE: I'm good at guessing. You'll not miss owt by coming with us to church, and we'll expect you at home tonight for a wedding-spread.

VICKEY: It's asking us to approve.

MAGGIE: You have approved. You've kissed the bridegroom and you'll go along with us. Father's safe where he is.

ALICE: And the shop?

MAGGIE: Tubby can see to the shop. And that reminds me. You *can* sell me something. There are some rings in that drawer there, Vickey.

VICKEY: Brass rings?

MAGGIE: Yes. I want one. That's the size. (*She holds up her wedding-ring finger.*)

VICKEY: That! But you're not taking it for—
     VICKEY *puts box of rings on the counter.*

MAGGIE: Yes, I am. Will and me aren't throwing money round, but we can pay our way. There's fourpence for the ring. Gather it up, Vickey. (*Putting down money and trying on rings.*)

ALICE: Wedded with a brass ring!

MAGGIE: This one will do. It's a nice fit. Alice, you haven't entered that sale in your book. No wonder you're worried with the accounts if that's the way you see to them. (*She puts ring in her bag.*)

ALICE: I'm a bit too much astonished at you to think about accounts. A ring out of stock!

MAGGIE: They're always out of someone's stock.

VICKEY: Well, I'd think shame to myself to be married with a ring like that.

MAGGIE: When folks can't afford the best they have to do without.

VICKEY: I'll take good care I never go without.

MAGGIE: Semi-detached for you, I suppose, and a houseful of new furniture.

ALICE: Haven't you furnished?

MAGGIE: Partly what. We've made a start at the Flat Iron Market.

ALICE: I'd stay single sooner than have other people's cast-off sticks in my house. Where's your pride gone to, Maggie?

MAGGIE: I'm not getting wed myself to help the furnishing trade along. I suppose you'd turn your nose up at second-hand stuff, too, Vickey?

VICKEY: I'd start properly or not at all.

MAGGIE: Then you'll neither of you have any objections to my clearing out the lumber-room upstairs. We've brought a hand-cart round with us.

WILL *takes his coat off. He has detachable cuffs which he places carefully on the arm-chair.*

VICKEY: You made sure of things.

MAGGIE: Yes. Get upstairs, Will. I told you what to bring.

ALICE: Wait a bit.

MAGGIE: Go on.

WILL *goes into the house.*

ALICE: Let me tell you if you claim the furniture from your old bedroom, that it's my room now, and you'll not budge a stick of it.

MAGGIE: I expected you'd promote yourself, Alice. But I said lumber-room. There's a two-three broken chairs in the attic and a sofa with the springs all gone. You'll not tell me they're of any use to you.

ALICE: Nor to you, neither.

MAGGIE: Will's handy with his fingers. He'll put in this afternoon mending them. They'll be secure against you come to sit on them at supper-time tonight.

VICKEY: And that's the way you're going to live! With cast-off furniture.

MAGGIE: Aye. In two cellars in Oldfield Road.

VICKEY *and* ALICE: A cellar!

MAGGIE: *Two* of 'em, Alice. One to live and work in and the other to sleep in.

ALICE: Well, it 'ud not suit me.

VICKEY: Nor me.

MAGGIE: It suits me fine. And when me and Will are richer than the lot of you together, it'll be a grand satisfaction to look back and think about how we were when we began.

WILL *appears with two crippled chairs and begins to cross the shop.*

VICKEY: Just a minute, Will. (*She examines the chairs.*) These chairs are not so bad.

MAGGIE: You can sit on one tonight and see.

VICKEY: You know, mended up, those chairs would do very well for my kitchen when I'm wed.

ALICE: Yes, or for mine.

MAGGIE: I reckon my parlour comes afront of your kitchens, though.

VICKEY: Parlour! I thought you said you'd only one living-room.

MAGGIE: Then it might as well be called a parlour as by any other name. (*Crosses to doors and opens them.*) Put the chairs on the hand-cart, Will.

    WILL *goes out to street.*

And as for your kitchens, you've got none yet, and if you want my plan for you to work, you'll just remember all I'm taking off you is some crippled stuff that isn't yours and what I'm getting for you is marriage portions.

ALICE: What?

VICKEY: Marriage portions, Maggie?

    FREDDY *re-enters, accompanied by* ALBERT.

MAGGIE (*to Vickey and Alice*): You'd better put your hats on now, or you'll be late at the church.

VICKEY: But aren't we to know first—?

MAGGIE (*herding them to exit*): You'll know all right. Be quick with your things now.

    ALICE *and* VICKEY *go out.*

MAGGIE (*turns*): Good morning, Albert. Have you got what Freddy asked you for?

ALBERT: Yes, but I'm afraid—

    WILL *re-enters from street.*

MAGGIE: Never mind being afraid. Freddy, I told you I'd a job here for you. You go upstairs with Will. There's a sofa to come down. Get your coat off to it. Now, then, Albert.

FREDDY: But—

MAGGIE: I've told you what to do, and you can't do it in your coat. If that sofa isn't here in two minutes, I'll leave the lot of you to tackle this yourselves and a nice hash you'll make of it.

    FREDDY *takes his coat off.*

FREDDY: All right, Maggie.

    FREDDY *goes out.* ALBERT *produces blue paper. She reads.*

MAGGIE: Do you call this English?

ALBERT: Legal English, Miss Hobson.

MAGGIE: I thought it weren't the sort we talk in Lancashire.

What is it when you've got behind the whereases and the saids and to wits?

ALBERT: It's what you told Freddy to instruct me. Action against Henry Horatio Hobson for trespass on the premises of Jonathan Beenstock & Co., Corn Merchants, of Chapel Street, Salford, with damages to certain corn bags caused by falling on them and further damages claimed for spying on the trade secrets of the aforesaid J. B. & Co.

MAGGIE: Well, I'll take your word that this means that – I shouldn't have thought it, but I suppose lawyers are like doctors. They've each a secret language of their own so that if you get a letter from one lawyer you've to take it to another to get it read, just like a doctor sends you to a chemist with a rigmarole that no one else can read, so they can charge you what they like for a drop of coloured water.

ALBERT: I've made this out to your instructions, Miss Hobson, but I'm far from saying it's good law, and I'd not be keen on going into court with it.

MAGGIE: Nobody asked you to. It won't come into court.

WILL *and* FREDDY *enter with a ramshackle horsehair sofa.*

Open that door for them, Albert.

ALBERT *opens street door. They pass out.*

What's the time? You can see the clock from there.

ALBERT (*outside street door*): It's a quarter to one.

MAGGIE (*flying to living-room door, opening it, and calling*): Girls, if you're late for my wedding I'll never forgive you.

She turns as WILL *and* FREDDY *return.*

Put your coats on. Now, then, Freddy, you take that paper and put it on *my* father in *your* cellar.

FREDDY: Now?

MAGGIE: Now? Yes, of course now. He might waken any time.

FREDDY: He looked fast enough. Aren't I to come to the church?

MAGGIE: Yes, if you do that quick enough to get there before we're through.

FREDDY: All right. (*He goes out, pocketing the paper.* MAGGIE *follows him to the door.*)

MAGGIE: Now there's that hand-cart. Are we to take it with us?

ALBERT: To church! You can't do that.

WILLIE: I'll take it home. (*Slight move.*)

MAGGIE: And have me waiting for you at the church? That's not for me, my lad.

ALBERT: You can't very well leave it where it is.

MAGGIE: No. There's only one thing for it. You'll have to take it to our place, Albert.

ALBERT: Me!

MAGGIE: There's the key. (*She hands it from her bag.*) It's 39a, Oldfield Road.

ALBERT: Yes, but to push a hand-cart through Salford in broad daylight!

MAGGIE: It won't dirty your collar.

ALBERT: Suppose some of my friends see me?

MAGGIE: Look here, my lad, if you're too proud to do a job like that, you're not the husband for my sister.

ALBERT: It's the look of the thing. Can't you send somebody from here?

MAGGIE: No. You can think it over. (*She raises trap.*) Tubby!

TUBBY (*below*): Yes, Miss. (*He appears half-way up trap.*) Why, it's Miss Maggie!

MAGGIE: Come up, Tubby. You're in charge of the shop. We'll all be out for awhile.

TUBBY: I'll be up in half a minute, Miss Maggie. (*He goes down and closes trap.*)

MAGGIE: Well, Albert Prosser?

ALBERT: I suppose I must.

MAGGIE: That's right. We'll call it your wedding gift to me, and I'll allow you're putting yourself out a bit for me.

Going with him to the door. He goes. She turns.
Well, Will, you've not had much to say for yourself today. Howst feeling, lad?

WILLIE: I'm going through with it, Maggie.

MAGGIE: Eh?

WILLIE: My mind's made up. I've got wrought up to point. I'm ready.

MAGGIE: It's church we're going to, not the dentist's.

WILLIE: I know. You get rid of summat at dentist's, but it's taking summat on to go to church with a wench, and the Lord knows what.

MAGGIE: Sithee, Will, I've a respect for church. Yon's not the place for lies. The parson's going to ask you will you have me and you'll either answer truthfully or not at all. If you're not willing, just say so now, and—

WILLIE: I'll tell him 'yes'.

MAGGIE: And truthfully?

WILLIE: Yes, Maggie. I'm resigned. You're growing on me, lass. I'll toe the line with you.

 ALICE *and* VICKEY *enter in their Sunday clothes – the same at which Hobson grew indignant in Act One.*

ALICE: We're ready, Maggie.

MAGGIE: And time you were. It's not your weddings that you're dressing for. (*By trap.*) Come up, Tubby, and keep an eye on things.

VICKEY (*to Will*): Will, have you got the ring?

MAGGIE: I have. Do you think I'd trust him to remember?

 MAGGIE *goes off with* WILL. VICKEY *and* ALICE *are following, laughing.* TUBBY *comes up trap and throws old shoes after them.*

CURTAIN

ACT THREE

The cellar in Oldfield Road is at once workroom, shop, and living-room. It is entered from the right corner by a door at the top of a flight of some seven stairs. Its three windows are high up at the back – not shop windows, but simply to give light. Each window has on it 'William Mossop, Practical Bootmaker', reversed as seen from the inside, and is illuminated dimly from outside by a neighbouring street lamp.

A door leads to the bedroom. Up stage left is a small screen or partition whose purpose is to conceal the sink. A shoemaker's bench, leather and tackle are against the wall, above the fire-place. Below the door, left, is a small dresser. Table centre. Seating accommodation consists solely of the sofa and the two chairs taken from Hobson's, now repaired. The sofa is left of the table. Crowded on the sofa are, in order, from down up, ALBERT, ALICE, VICKEY, FRED.

As the curtain rises, the four are standing, tea-cups in hand, saying together: 'The Bride and Bridegroom.' *They drink and sit. General laughter and conversation. On the chair down stage is* MAGGIE. *From the other chair, centre, behind table,* WILL *rises, nervously, and rushes his little speech like a child who has learnt a lesson. The table has hot-house flowers (in a basin) and the remains of a meal at which tea only has been drunk, and the feast is represented by the sections of a large pork pie and a small wedding cake. As* WILL *rises,* ALBERT *hammers on the table.* ALICE *suppresses him.*

WILLIE: It's a very great pleasure to us to see you here tonight. It's an honour you do us, and I assure you, speaking

39

for my – my wife, as well as for myself, that the – the—

MAGGIE (*in an undertone*): Generous.

WILLIE: Oh, aye. That's it. That the generous warmth of the sentiments so cordially expressed by Mr Beenstock and so enthusiastically seconded by – no, I've gotten that wrong road round – expressed by Mr Prosser and seconded by Mr Beenstock – will never be forgotten by either my life partner or self – and – and I'd like to drink this toast to you in my own house. Our guests, and may they all be married soon themselves.

MAGGIE (*rising and drinking with Will*): Our guests.

　　WILL *and* MAGGIE *sit. General laughter and conversation.*

ALBERT (*solemnly rising*): In rising to respond—

ALICE (*tugging his coat and pulling him into his seat*): Sit down. We've had enough of speeches. I know men fancy themselves when they're talking, but you've had one turn and you needn't start again.

ALBERT: But we ought to thank him, Alice.

ALICE: I dare say. But you'll not speak as well as he did, so we can leave it with a good wind-up. I'm free to own you took me by surprise, Will.

FREDDY: Very neat speech indeed.

VICKEY: Who taught you, Will?

WILLIE: I've been learning a lot lately.

ALICE: I thought that speech never came natural from Will.

MAGGIE: I'm educating him.

FREDDY: Very apt pupil, I must say.

MAGGIE: He'll do. Another twenty years and I know which of you three men 'ull be thought most of at the Bank.

FREDDY: That's looking ahead a bit.

MAGGIE: I'll admit it needs imagination to see it now.

ALBERT: Well, the start's all right, you know. Snug little rooms. Shop of your own. And so on. I was wondering where you raised the capital for this, Maggie.

MAGGIE: I? You mustn't call it my shop. It's his.

ALICE: Do you mean to tell me that Willie found the capital?

MAGGIE: He's the saving sort.

ALICE: He must be if you've done this out of what father used to pay him.

MAGGIE: Well, we haven't. Not altogether. We've had help.

ALBERT: Ah!

VICKEY: It's a mystery to me where you got it from.

MAGGIE: Same place as those flowers, Albert.

ALBERT: Hot-house flowers, I see. (*He rises and examines them.*) I was wondering where they came from.

    VICKEY *and* FREDDY *smell flowers.*

MAGGIE: Same place as the money, Albert.

ALBERT: Ah!

ALICE (*rising*): Well, I think we ought to be getting home, Maggie.

MAGGIE (*rising, as do the rest*): I shouldn't marvel. I reckon Tubby's a bit tired of looking after the shop by now, and if father's wakened up and come in—

ALICE: That's it. I'm a bit nervous.

MAGGIE: He'll have an edge on his temper. Come and put your hats on.

    She is going with ALICE *and* VICKEY, *then stops.*

    Willie, we'll need this table when they're gone. You'd better be clearing the pots away.

WILLIE: Yes, Maggie.

FREDDY: But – you—

ALBERT: Oh, Lord!

    They laugh.

MAGGIE (*quite calmly*): And you and Fred can just lend him a hand with the washing-up, Albert.

FREDDY: Me wash pots!

VICKEY (*really outraged*): Maggie, we're guests.

MAGGIE: I know. Only Albert laughed at Willie, and washing up 'ull maybe make him think on that it's not allowed.

    She ushers ALICE *and* VICKEY *out, and follows.* WILLIE

begins to put pots on tray which he gets from behind screen.

ALBERT (*after he and Fred have looked at each other, then at Will, then at each other again*): Are you going to wash up pots?

FREDDY: Are you?

ALBERT: I look at it like this myself. All being well, you and I are marrying into this family and we know what Maggie is. If we start giving in to her now, she'll be a nuisance to us all our lives.

FREDDY: That's right enough, but there's this plan of hers to get us married. Are you prepared to work it for us?

ALBERT: I'm not. Anything but—

FREDDY: Then till she's done it we're to keep the sweet side of Maggie.

ALBERT: But, washing pots!

There is a pause. They look at Will, who has brought the tray from behind the screen and is now clearing up the table.

FREDDY: What would you do in our place, Will?

WILLIE: Please yourselves. I'm getting on with what she told me.

FREDDY: You're married to her. We aren't.

ALBERT: What do you need the table for in such a hurry?

WILLIE: Nay, I'm not in any hurry myself.

FREDDY: Maggie wants it for something.

WILLIE: It'll be for my lessons, I reckon. She's schooling me.

FREDDY: And don't you want to learn, then?

WILLIE: 'Tisn't that. I – just don't want to be rude to you – turning you out so early. I don't see you need to go away so soon.

ALBERT: Why not?

WILLIE: I'm fond of a bit of company.

ALBERT: Do you want company on your wedding night?

WILLIE: I don't favour your going so soon.

FREDDY: He's afraid to be alone with her. That's what it is. He's shy of his wife.

They laugh.

WILLIE: That's a fact. I've not been married before, you see. I've not been left alone with her, either. Up to now she's been coming round to where I lodged at Tubby Wadlow's to give me my lessons. It's different now, and I freely own I'm feeling awkward-like. I'd be deeply obliged if you would stay on a bit to help to – to thaw the ice for me.

FREDDY: You've been engaged to her, haven't you?

WILLIE: Aye, but it weren't for long. And you see, Maggie's not the sort you get familiar with.

FREDDY: You had quite long enough to thaw the ice. It's not our job to do your melting for you.

ALBERT: No. Fred, these pots need washing. We will wash them.

ALBERT *carries tray behind screen. Water runs. He is seen flourishing towels.* FRED *is following when* WILLIE *calls him back and takes tray to table.*

WILLIE: Fred, would you like it yourself with – with a wench like Maggie?

FREDDY: That's not the point. It wasn't me she married.

WILLIE: It's that being alone with her that worries me, and I did think you'd stand by a fellow man to make things not so strange at first.

ALBERT: That's not the way we look at it. Hurry up with those cups, Fred.

MAGGIE *enters with* VICKEY *and* ALICE *in outdoor clothes.*

MAGGIE: Have you broken anything yet, Albert?

ALBERT (*indignantly*): Broken? No. (*Takes cup from tray and wipes it.*)

MAGGIE: Too slow to, I expect.

FREDDY: I must say you don't show much gratitude.

ALBERT: Aren't you at all surprised to find us doing this?

MAGGIE: Surprised? I told you to do it.

FREDDY: Yes, but—

MAGGIE (*taking towel from him*): You can stop now. I'll finish when you're gone.

Knock at door upstairs.

ALICE: Who's that?

MAGGIE: Someone who can't read, I reckon. You hung that card on door, Will?

WILLIE: Aye, it's there. And you wrote it, Maggie.

MAGGIE: I knew better than to trust to you. 'Business suspended for the day' it says, and they that can't read it can go on knocking.

HOBSON (*off, upstairs, after another knock*): Are you in, Maggie?

VICKEY (*terrified*): It's father!

ALBERT: Oh, Lord!

MAGGIE: What's the matter? Are you afraid of him?

FREDDY: Well, I think, all things considered, and seeing—

MAGGIE: All right. We'll consider 'em. You can go into the bedroom, the lot of you. . . . No, not you, Willie. The rest. I'll shout when I want you.

ALICE: When he's gone.

MAGGIE: It'll be before he's gone.

VICKEY: But we don't want—

MAGGIE: Is this your house or mine?

VICKEY: It's your cellar.

MAGGIE: And I'm in charge of it.

The four go into bedroom. VICKEY *starts to argue.* ALBERT *opens the door.* VICKEY *and* ALICE *go out followed by* FREDDY *and* ALBERT. VICKEY *is pushed inside.* WILL *is going to stairs.* You sit you still, and don't forget you're gaffer here. I'll open door.

WILLIE *sits in chair above table.* MAGGIE *goes upstairs and opens the door. Enter* HOBSON *to top stair.*

HOBSON (*with some slight apology*): Well, Maggie.

MAGGIE (*uninvitingly*): Well, father.

HOBSON (*without confidence*): I'll come in.

MAGGIE (*standing in his way*): Well, I don't know. I'll have to ask the master about that.

HOBSON: Eh? The master?

MAGGIE: You and him didn't part on the best of terms, you know. (*Over the railings.*) Will, it's my father. Is he to come in?

WILLIE (*loudly and boldly*): Aye, let him come.

HOBSON *comes downstairs.* MAGGIE *closes door behind him and follows.* HOBSON *stares round at the cellar.*

HOBSON: You don't sound cordial about your invitation, young man.

WILLIE: Nay, but I am. (*Shaking hands for a long time.*) I'm right down glad to see you, Mr Hobson. It makes the wedding-day complete-like, you being her father and I – I hope you'll see your way to staying a good long while.

HOBSON: Well—

MAGGIE: That's enough, Will. You don't need to overdo it. You can sit down for five minutes, father. That sofa 'ull bear your weight. It's been tested.

WILLIE (*taking up teapot*): There's nobbut tea to drink and I reckon what's in the pot is stewed, so I'll—

MAGGIE (*taking pot off him as he moves to fire-place with it*): You'll not do owt of sort. Father likes his liquids strong.

WILLIE: A piece of pork pie now, Mr Hobson?

HOBSON (*groaning*): Pork pie!

MAGGIE (*sharply*): You'll be sociable now you're here, I hope. (*She pours tea at table, top end.*)

HOBSON: It wasn't sociability that brought me, Maggie.

MAGGIE: What was it, then?

HOBSON: Maggie, I'm in disgrace. A sore and sad misfortune's fallen on me.

MAGGIE (*cutting*): Happen a piece of wedding cake 'ull do you good.

HOBSON (*shuddering*): It's sweet.

MAGGIE: That's natural in cake.

MAGGIE *sits in chair above table.*

HOBSON: I've gotten such a head.

MAGGIE: Aye. But wedding cake's a question of heart. There'd be no bride cakes made at all if we thought first about our heads. I'm quite aware it's foolishness, but I've a wish to see my father sitting at my table eating my wedding cake on my wedding-day.

HOBSON: It's a very serious thing I came about, Maggie.

MAGGIE: It's not more serious than knowing that you wish us well.

HOBSON: Well, Maggie, you know my way. When a thing's done it's done. You've had your way and done what you wanted. I'm none proud of the choice you made and I'll not lie and say I am, but I've shaken your husband's hand, and that's a sign for you. The milk's spilt and I'll not cry.

MAGGIE (*holding plate*): Then there's your cake, and you can eat it.

HOBSON: I've given you my word there's no ill feeling. (*Pushes cake away.*)

MAGGIE: So now we'll have the deed. (*Pushes it back.*)

HOBSON: You're a hard woman. (*He eats.*) You've no consideration for the weakness of old age.

MAGGIE: Finished?

HOBSON: Pass me that tea.

She passes: he drinks.

That's easier.

MAGGIE: Now tell me what it is you came about?

HOBSON: I'm in sore trouble, Maggie.

MAGGIE (*rising and going towards the door*): Then I'll leave you with my husband to talk it over.

HOBSON: Eh?

MAGGIE: You'll not be wanting me. Women are only in your way.

HOBSON (*rising*): Maggie, you're not going to desert me in the hour of my need, are you?

MAGGIE: Surely to goodness you don't want a woman to help you after all you've said! Will 'ull do his best, I make no doubt. (*She goes towards door.*) Give me a call when you've finished, Will.

HOBSON (*following her*): Maggie! It's private.

MAGGIE: Why, yes. I'm going and you can discuss it man to man with no fools of women about.

HOBSON: I tell you I've come to see you, not him. It's private from him.

MAGGIE: Private from Will? Nay, it isn't. Will's in the family and you've nowt to say to me that can't be said to him.

HOBSON: I've to tell you this with him there?

MAGGIE: Will and me's one.

WILLIE: Sit down, Mr Hobson.

MAGGIE: You call him father now.

WILLIE (*astonished*): Do I?

HOBSON: Does he?

MAGGIE: He does. Sit down, Will.

WILL *sits right of table.* MAGGIE *stands at the head of the table.* HOBSON *sits on sofa.*

Now, if you're ready, father, we are. What's the matter?

HOBSON: That – (*producing the blue paper*) – that's the matter.

MAGGIE *accepts and passes it to Will and goes behind his chair. He is reading upside down. She bends over chair and turns it right way up.*

MAGGIE: What is it, Will?

HOBSON (*banging on table*): Ruin, Maggie, that's what it is! Ruin and bankruptcy. Am I vicar's warden at St Philip's or am I not? Am I Hobson of Hobson's Boot Shop on Chapel Street, Salford? Am I a respectable ratepayer and the father of a family or—

MAGGIE (*who has been reading over Will's shoulder*): It's an action for damages for trespass, I see.

HOBSON: It's a stab in the back; it's an unfair, un-English, cowardly way of taking a mean advantage of a casual accident.

MAGGIE: Did you trespass?

HOBSON: Maggie, I say it solemnly, it is all your fault. I had an accident. I don't deny it. I'd been in the 'Moonraker's' and I'd stayed too long. And why? Why did I stay too long? To try to forget that I'd a thankless child, to erase from the tablets of memory the recollection of your conduct. That was the cause of it. And the result, the blasting, withering result? I fell into that cellar. I slept in that cellar and I awoke to this catastrophe. Lawyers . . . law-costs . . . publicity . . . ruin.

MAGGIE: I'm still asking you. Was it an accident? Or did you trespass?

HOBSON: It's an accident. As plain as Salford Town Hall it's an accident, but they that live by law have twisted ways of putting things that make white show as black. I'm in their grip at last. I've kept away from lawyers all my life, I've hated lawyers, and they've got their chance to make me bleed for it. I've dodged them, and they've caught me in the end. They'll squeeze me dry for it.

WILLIE: My word, and that's summat like a squeeze and all.

     HOBSON *stares at him*.

MAGGIE: I can see it's serious. I shouldn't wonder if you didn't lose some trade from this.

HOBSON: Wonder! It's as certain as Christmas. My good-class customers are not going to buy their boots from a man who's stood up in open court and had to acknowledge he was overcome at 12 o'clock in the morning. They'll not remember it was private grief that caused it all. They'll only think the worse of me because I couldn't control my daughter better than to let her go and be the cause of sorrow to me in my age. That's what you've done. Brought this on me, you two, between you.

WILLIE: Do you think it will get into the paper, Maggie?

MAGGIE: Yes, for sure. You'll see your name in the *Salford Reporter*, father.

HOBSON: *Salford Reporter!* Yes, and more. When there is ruin and disaster, and outrageous fortune overwhelms a man of my importance to the world, it isn't only the *Salford Reporter* that takes note of it. This awful cross that's come to me will be recorded in the *Manchester Guardian* for the whole of Lancashire to read.

WILLIE: Eh, by gum, think of that! To have your name appearing in the *Guardian*! Why, it's very near worth while to be ruined for the pleasure of reading about yourself in a printed paper.

HOBSON (*sits sofa*): It's there for others to read besides me, my lad.

WILLIE: Aye, you're right. I didn't think of that. This 'ull give a lot of satisfaction to a many I could name. Other people's troubles is mostly what folks read the paper for, and I reckon it's twice the pleasure to them when it's trouble of a man they know themselves. (*He is perfectly simple and has no malicious intention.*)

HOBSON: To hear you talk it sounds like a pleasure to you.

WILLIE (*sincerely*): Nay, it's not. You've ate my wedding cake and you've shook my hand. We're friends, I hope, and I were nobbut meditating like a friend. I always think it's best to look on the worst side of things first, then whatever chances can't be worse than you looked for. There's St Philip's now. I don't suppose you'll go on being vicar's warden after this to do, and it brought you a powerful lot of customers from the church, did that.

HOBSON (*turning to her*): I'm getting a lot of comfort from your husband, Maggie.

MAGGIE: It's about what you deserve.

HOBSON: Have you got any more consolation for me, Will?

WILLIE (*aggrieved*): I only spoke what came into my mind.

HOBSON: Well, have you spoken it all?

WILLIE: I can keep my mouth shut if you'd rather.

HOBSON: Don't strain yourself, Will Mossop. When a man's

mind is full of thoughts like yours, they're better out than in. You let them come, lad. They'll leave a cleaner place behind.

WILLIE: I'm not much good at talking, and I always seem to say wrong things when I do talk. I'm sorry if my well-meant words don't suit your taste, but I thought you came here for advice.

HOBSON: I didn't come to you, you jumped-up cock-a-hooping— (*Rising.*)

MAGGIE: That 'ull do, father. (*Pushes him down.*) My husband's *trying* to help you.

HOBSON (*glares impatiently for a time, then meekly says*): Yes, Maggie.

MAGGIE: Now about this accident of yours.

HOBSON: Yes, Maggie.

MAGGIE: It's the publicity that you're afraid of most.

HOBSON: It's being dragged into a court of law at all, me that's voted right all through my life and been a sound supporter of the Queen and Constitution.

MAGGIE: Then we must try to keep it out of court.

HOBSON: If there are lawyers in Heaven, Maggie, which I doubt, they may keep cases out of courts there. On earth a lawyer's job's to squeeze a man and squeeze him where his squirming's seen the most – in court.

MAGGIE: I've heard of cases being settled out of court, in private.

HOBSON: In private? Yes, I dare say, and all the worse for that. It's done amongst themselves in lawyers' offices behind closed doors so no one can see they're squeezing twice as hard in private as they'd dare to do in public. There's some restraint demanded by a public place, but privately! It'll cost a fortune to settle this in private, Maggie.

MAGGIE: I make no doubt it's going to cost you something, but you'd rather do it privately than publicly?

HOBSON: If only it were not a lawyer's office.

MAGGIE: You can settle it with the lawyer out of his office. You can settle with him here.

She goes and opens door.

Albert!

Enter ALBERT, *who leaves door open.*

This is Mr Prosser, of Prosser, Pilkington, and Prosser.

HOBSON (*amazed*): He is!

MAGGIE: Yes.

HOBSON (*incredulously, rising*): You're a lawyer?

ALBERT: Yes, I'm a lawyer.

HOBSON (*with disgust almost too deep for words*): At your age!

MAGGIE (*going up to door*): Come out, all of you.

There is reluctance inside, then VICKEY, ALICE *and* FRED *enter and stand in a row.*

HOBSON: Alice! Vickey!

MAGGIE: Family gathering. This is Mr Beenstock, of Beenstock & Co.

FREDDY: How do you do?

HOBSON: What! Here!

The situation is plainly beyond his mused brain's capacity.

MAGGIE: When you've got a thing to settle, you need all the parties to be present.

HOBSON: But there are so many of them. Where have they all come from?

MAGGIE: My bedroom.

HOBSON: Your—? Maggie, I wish you'd explain before my brain gives way.

MAGGIE: It's quite simple. I got them here because I expected you.

HOBSON: You expected me!

MAGGIE: Yes. You're in trouble.

HOBSON (*shaking his head, then as if finding an outlet, pouncing on Alice*): What's it got to do with Alice and Vickey? What are they doing here? What's happening to the shop?

ALICE: Tubby Wadlow's looking after it.

HOBSON: And is it Tubby's job to look after the shop?

VICKEY: He'd got no other job. The shop's so slack since Maggie left.

HOBSON (*swelling with rage*): And do you run that shop? Do you give orders there? Do you decide when you can put your hats on and walk out of it?

MAGGIE: They come out because it's my wedding-day, father. It's reason enough, and Will and me 'ull do the same for them. We'll close the shop and welcome on their wedding-days.

HOBSON: Their wedding-days! That's a long time off. It'll be many a year before there's another wedding in this family, I give you my word. (*Turns to Maggie.*) One daughter defying me is quite enough.

ALBERT: Hadn't we better get to business, sir?

HOBSON (*turning on him*): Young man, don't abuse a noble word. You're a lawyer. By your own admission you're a lawyer. Honest men live by business and lawyers live by law.

ALBERT: In this matter, sir, I am following the instructions of my client, Mr Beenstock, and the remark you have just let fall, before witnesses, appears to me to bear a libellous reflection on the action of my client.

HOBSON: What! So it's libel now. Isn't trespass and . . . and spying on trade secrets enough for you, you blood-sucking—

ALBERT: One moment, Mr Hobson. You can call me what you like—

HOBSON: And I shall. You—

ALBERT: But I wish to remind you, in your own interests, that abuse of a lawyer is remembered in the costs. Now, my client tells me he is prepared to settle this matter out of court. Personally, I don't advise him to, because we should probably get higher damages in court. But Mr Beenstock has no desire to be vindictive. He remembers your position, your reputation for respectability, and—

HOBSON: How much?

ALBERT: Er – I beg your pardon?

HOBSON: I'm not so fond of the sound of your voice as you are. What's the figure?

ALBERT: The sum we propose, which will include my ordinary costs, but not any additional costs incurred by your use of defamatory language to me, is one thousand pounds.

HOBSON: What!

MAGGIE: It isn't.

HOBSON: One thousand pounds for tumbling down a cellar! Why, I might have broken my leg.

ALBERT: That is in the nature of an admission, Mr Hobson. Our flour bags saved your legs from fracture and I am therefore inclined to add to the sum I have stated a reasonable estimate of the doctor's bill we have saved you by protecting your legs with our bags.

MAGGIE: Eh, Albert Prosser, I can see you're going to get on in the world, but you needn't be greedy here. That one thousand's too much.

ALBERT: We thought—

MAGGIE: Then you can think again.

FREDDY: But—

MAGGIE: If there are any more signs of greediness from you two, there'll be a counter-action for personal damages due to your criminal carelessness in leaving your cellar flap open.

HOBSON: Maggie, you've saved me. I'll bring that action. I'll show them up.

MAGGIE: You're not damaged, and one lawyer's quite enough. But he'll be more reasonable now. I know perfectly well what father can afford to pay, and it's not a thousand pounds nor anything like a thousand pounds.

HOBSON: Not so much of your can't afford, Maggie. You'll make me out a pauper.

MAGGIE: You can afford five hundred pounds and you're going to pay five hundred pounds.

HOBSON: Oh, but . . . there's a difference between affording and paying.

MAGGIE: You can go to the courts and be reported in the papers if you like.

HOBSON: It's the principle I care about. I'm being beaten by a lawyer.

VICKEY: Father, dear, how can you be beaten when they wanted a thousand pounds and you're only going to give five hundred pounds?

HOBSON: I hadn't thought of that.

VICKEY: It's they who are beaten.

HOBSON: I'd take a good few beatings myself at the price, Vickey. Still, I want this keeping out of court.

ALBERT: Then we can take it as settled?

HOBSON: Do you want to see the money before you believe me? Is that your nasty lawyer's way?

ALBERT: Not at all, Mr Hobson. Your word is as good as your bond.

VICKEY: It's settled! It's settled! Hurrah! Hurrah!

HOBSON: Well, I don't see what you have to cheer about, Vickey. I'm not to be dragged to public scorn, but you know this is a tidy bit of money to be going out of the family.

MAGGIE: It's not going out of the family, father.

HOBSON: I don't see how you make it out.

MAGGIE: Their wedding-day is not so far off as you thought, now there's the half of five hundred pounds apiece for them to make a start on.

ALBERT *and* ALICE, FRED *and* VICKEY *stand arm in arm.*

HOBSON: You mean to tell me—

MAGGIE: You won't forget you've passed your word, will you, father?

HOBSON (*rising*): I've been diddled. It's a plant. It—

MAGGIE: It takes two daughters off your hands at once, and

clears your shop of all the fools of women that used to lumber up the place.

ALICE: It will be much easier for you without us in your way, father.

HOBSON: Aye, and you can keep out of my way and all. Do you hear that, all of you?

VICKEY: Father . . .!

HOBSON (*picking up his hat*): I'll run that shop with men and – and I'll show Salford how it should be run. Don't you imagine there'll be room for you when you come home crying and tired of your fine husbands. I'm rid of ye, and it's a lasting riddance, mind. I'll pay this money, that you've robbed me of, and that's the end of it. All of you. You, especially, Maggie. I'm not blind yet, and I can see who 'tis I've got to thank for this. (*He goes to foot of stairs.*)

MAGGIE: Don't be vicious, father.

HOBSON: Will Mossop, I'm sorry for you. (*Over banisters.*) Take you for all in all, you're the best of the bunch. You're a backward lad, but you know your trade and it's an honest one.

HOBSON *is going up the stairs.*

ALICE: So does my Albert know his trade.

HOBSON (*half-way up stairs*): I'll grant you that. He knows his trade. He's good at robbery. (ALICE *shows great indignation.*) And I've to have it on my conscience that my daughter's wed a lawyer and an employer of lawyers.

VICKEY: It didn't worry your conscience to keep us serving in the shop at no wages.

HOBSON: I kept you, didn't I? It's someone else's job to victual you in future. Aye, you may grin, you two, but girls don't live on air. Your penny buns 'ull cost you tuppence now – and more. Wait till the families begin to come. Don't come to me for keep, that's all. (*Going.*)

ALICE: Father!

HOBSON (*turning*): Aye, you may father me. But that's a

piece of work I've finished with. I've done with fathering, and they're beginning it. They'll know what marrying a woman means before so long. They're putting chains upon themselves and I have thrown the shackles off. I've suffered thirty years and more and I'm a free man from today. Lord, what a thing you're taking on! You poor, poor wretches. You're red-nosed robbers, but you're going to pay for it.

He opens door and exits.

MAGGIE: You'd better arrange to get married quick. Alice and Vickey will have a sweet time with him.

FREDDY: Can they go home at all?

MAGGIE: Why not?

FREDDY: After what he said?

MAGGIE: He'll not remember half of it. He's for the 'Moonraker's' now – if there's time. What is the time?

ALBERT: Time we were going, Maggie; you'll be glad to see the back of us. (*He shows Maggie his watch.*)

WILLIE: No. No. I wouldn't dream of asking you to go.

MAGGIE (*moving up to get hats*): Then I would. It's high time we turned you out. There are your hats.

She gets Albert's and Fred's hats from rack.

Good night.

ALBERT *and* FREDDY *go upstairs.*

Good night, Vickey.

VICKEY (*with a quick kiss*): Good night, Maggie.

VICKEY *goes upstairs. She and* FREDDY *go out.*

MAGGIE: Good night, Alice.

ALICE: Good night, Maggie. (*The same quick kiss.*) And thank you.

MAGGIE: Oh, that! (*She goes with her to stairs.*) I'll see you again soon, only don't come round here too much, because Will and me's going to be busy and you'll maybe find enough to do yourselves with getting wed.

ALICE: I dare say. (*Upstairs.*)

The general exit is continuous, punctuated with laughter and merry 'Good nights!'

MAGGIE: Send us word when the day is.

ALBERT: We'll be glad to see you at the wedding.

MAGGIE: We'll come to that. You'll be too grand for us afterwards.

ALBERT: Oh, no, Maggie.

MAGGIE: Well, happen we'll be catching up with you before so long. We're only starting here. Good night.

ALBERT ⎫
ALICE ⎭ : Good night, Maggie.

They go out, closing door. MAGGIE *turns to Will, putting her hands on his shoulders. He starts.*

MAGGIE: Now you've heard what I've said of you tonight. In twenty years you're going to be thought more of than either of your brothers-in-law.

WILLIE: I heard you say it, Maggie.

MAGGIE: And we're to make it good. I'm not a boaster, Will. And it's to be in less than twenty years, and all.

WILLIE: Well, I dunno. They've a long start on us.

MAGGIE: And you've got me. Your slate's in the bedroom. Bring it out. I'll have this table clear by the time you come back.

She hustles off the last remains of the meal, putting the flowers on the mantel and takes off cloth, placing it over the back of a chair. WILL *goes to bedroom and returns with a slate and slate pencil. The slate is covered with writing. He puts it on table.*

MAGGIE: Off with your Sunday coat now. You don't want to make a mess of that.

He takes coat off and gets rag from behind screen and brings it back to table.

What are you doing with that mopping rag?

WILLIE: I was going to wash out what's on the slate.

MAGGIE: Let me see it first. That's what you did last night at Tubby's after I came here?

WILLIE: Yes, Maggie.

MAGGIE (*reading*): 'There is always room at the top.' (*Washing it out.*) Your writing's improving, Will. I'll set you a short copy for tonight, because it's getting late and we've a lot to do in the morning. (*Writing.*) 'Great things grow from small.' Now, then, you can sit down here and copy that.

He takes her place at the table. MAGGIE *watches a moment, then goes to fire-place and fingers the flowers.*

I'll put these flowers of Mrs Hepworth's behind the fire, Will. We'll not want litter in the place come working time tomorrow.

She takes up basin, stops, looks at WILL, *who is bent over his slate, and takes a flower out, throwing the rest behind the fire and going to bedroom with one.*

WILLIE (*looking up*): You're saving one.

MAGGIE (*caught in an act of sentiment and apologetically*): I thought I'd press it in my Bible for a keepsake, Will. I'm not beyond liking to be reminded of this day.

She looks at screen and yawns.

Lord, I'm tired. I reckon I'll leave those pots till morning. It's a slackish way of starting, but I don't get married every day.

WILLIE (*industrious at his slate*): No.

MAGGIE: I'm for my bed. You finish that copy before you come.

WILLIE: Yes, Maggie.

Exit MAGGIE *to bedroom, with the flower. She closes door.* WILL *copies, repeats letters and words as he writes them slowly, finishes, then rises and rakes out fire. He looks shyly at bedroom door, sits and takes his boots off. He rises, boots in hand, moves towards door, hesitates, and turns back, puts boots down at door, then returns to table and takes off his collar. Then hesitates again, finally makes up his mind, puts out light, and lies down on sofa with occasional glances at the bedroom door. At first he faces the fire. He is uncomfortable. He turns over and faces the door. In a minute* MAGGIE *opens the bedroom door. She has a candle and is in a plain calico night-dress. She comes to* WILL, *shines the light on him, takes him by the ear, and returns with him to bedroom.*

CURTAIN

ACT FOUR

*The scene represents Hobson's living-room, the door to which was
seen in Act One. From inside the room that door is now seen to be
at the left, the opposite wall having the fire-place and another door
to the house.*

It is eight o'clock on a morning a year later.

*In front of the fire-place is a horsehair arm-chair. Chairs to
match are at the table. There are coloured prints of Queen Victoria
and the Prince Consort on the walls on each side of the door at the
back, and a plain one of Lord Beaconsfield over the fire-place. Anti-
macassars abound, and the decoration is quaintly ugly. It is an
overcrowded, 'cosy' room. Hobson is quite contented with it,
and doesn't realize that it is at present very dirty.*

There is probably a kitchen elsewhere, but TUBBY WADLOW
*is cooking bacon at the fire. He is simultaneously laying breakfast
for one on the table. At both proceedings he is a puzzled and
incompetent amateur. Presently the left door opens, and* JIM
HEELER *appears.*

JIM (*crossing*): I'll go straight up to him, Tubby.

TUBBY (*checking him*): He's getting up, Mr Heeler.

JIM: Getting up! Why, you said—

TUBBY: I told you what he told me to tell you. Run for Doctor
MacFarlane, he said. And I ran for Doctor MacFarlane. Now
go to Mr Heeler, he said, and tell him I'm very ill, and I came
and told you. Then he said he would get up, and I was to
have his breakfast ready for him, and he'd see you down
here.

JIM: Nonsense, Tubby. Of course, I'll go up to him.

TUBBY: You know what he is, sir. I'll get blamed if you go, and he's short-tempered this morning.

JIM: I don't want to get you into trouble, Tubby. (*He sits.*)

TUBBY: Thank you, Mr Heeler.

JIM: I quite thought it was something serious.

TUBBY: If you ask me, it is.

JIM: Which way?

TUBBY: Every way you look at it. Mr Hobson's not his own old self, and the shop's not its own old self, and look at me. Now I ask you, Mr Heeler, man to man, is this work for a foreman shoe hand? Cooking and laying tables and—

JIM: By all accounts there's not much else for you to do.

TUBBY: There's better things than being a housemaid, if it's only making clogs.

JIM: They tell me clogs are a cut line.

TUBBY: Well, what are you to do? There's nothing else wanted. Hobson's in a bad way, and I'm telling no secret when I say it. It's fact that's known.

JIM: It's a thousand pities with an old-established trade like this.

TUBBY: And who's to blame?

JIM: I don't think you ought to discuss that with me, Tubby.

TUBBY: Don't you? I'm an old servant of the master's, and I'm sticking to him now when everybody's calling me a doting fool because I don't look after Tubby Wadlow first, and if that don't give me the right to say what I please, I don't know. It's temper's ruining this shop, Mr Heeler. Temper and obstinacy.

JIM: They say in Chapel Street it's Willie Mossop.

TUBBY: Willie's a good lad, though I say it that trained him. He hit us hard, did Willie, but we'd have got round that in time. With care, you understand, and tact. Tact. That's what the gaffer lacks. Miss Maggie, now . . . well, she's a marvel, aye, a fair knock-out. Not slavish, mind you. Stood up to the customers all the time, but she'd a way with her that sold the goods and made them come again for more. Look at us now. Men assistants in the shop.

JIM: Cost more than women.

TUBBY: Cost? They'd be dear at any price. Look here, Mr Heeler, take yourself. When you go to buy a pair of boots do you like to be tried on by a man or a nice soft young woman?

JIM: Well—

TUBBY: There you are. Stands to reason. It's human nature.

JIM: But there are two sides to that, Tubby. Look at the other.

TUBBY: Ladies?

JIM: Yes.

TUBBY: Ladies that are ladies wants trying on by their own sex, and them that aren't buys clogs. It's the good-class trade that pays, and Hobson's have lost it.

Enter HOBSON, *unshaven, without collar.*

JIM (*with cheerful sympathy*): Well, Henry!

HOBSON (*with acute melancholy and self-pity*): Oh, Jim! Oh, Jim! Oh, Jim!

TUBBY: Will you sit on the arm-chair by the fire or at the table?

HOBSON: The table? Breakfast? Bacon? Bacon, and I'm like this.

JIM assists him to arm-chair.

JIM: When a man's like this he wants a woman about the house, Henry.

HOBSON (*sitting*): I'll want then.

TUBBY: Shall I go for Miss Maggie, sir? – Mrs Mossop, I mean.

JIM: I think your daughters should be here.

HOBSON: They should. Only they're not. They're married, and I'm deserted by them all and I'll die deserted, then perhaps they'll be sorry for the way they've treated me. Tubby, have you got no work to do in the shop?

TUBBY: I might find some if I looked hard.

HOBSON: Then go and look. And take that bacon with you. I don't like the smell.

TUBBY (*getting bacon*): Are you sure you wouldn't like Miss Maggie here? I'll go for her and— (*He holds the bacon very close to Hobson's face.*)

HOBSON: Oh, go for her. Go for the devil. What does it matter who you go for? I'm a dying man.

TUBBY *takes bacon and goes out.*

JIM: What's all this talk about dying, Henry?

HOBSON: Oh, Jim! Oh, Jim! I've sent for the doctor. We'll know soon how near the end is.

JIM: Well, this is very sudden. You've never been ill in your life.

HOBSON: It's been saved up, and all come now at once.

JIM: What are your symptoms, Henry?

HOBSON: I'm all one symptom, head to foot. I'm frightened of myself, Jim. That's worst. You *would* call me a clean man, Jim?

JIM: Clean? Of course I would. Clean in body and mind.

HOBSON: I'm dirty now. I haven't washed this morning. Couldn't face the water. The only use I saw for water was to drown myself. The same with shaving. I've thrown my razor through the window. Had to or I'd have cut my throat.

JIM: Oh, come, come.

HOBSON: It's awful. I'll never trust myself again. I'm going to grow a beard – if I live.

JIM: You'll cheat the undertaker, Henry, but I fancy a doctor could improve you. What do you reckon is the cause of it now?

HOBSON: 'Moonraker's'.

JIM: You don't think—

HOBSON: I don't think. I know. I've seen it happen to others, but I never thought that it would come to me.

JIM: Nor me, neither. You're not a toper, Henry. I grant you're regular, but you don't exceed. It's a hard thing if a man can't take a drop of ale without its getting back at him like this. Why, it might be my turn next.

TUBBY *enters, showing in* DOCTOR MACFARLANE, *a domineering Scotsman of fifty.*

TUBBY: Here's Doctor MacFarlane.

Exit TUBBY.

DOCTOR: Good morning, gentlemen. Where's my patient? (*He puts hat on table.*)

JIM (*speaking without indicating Hobson*): Here. (*He does not rise.*)

DOCTOR: Here? Up?

HOBSON: Looks like it.

DOCTOR: And for a patient who's downstairs I'm made to rise from my bed at this hour?

JIM: It's not so early as all that.

DOCTOR: But I've been up all night, sir. Young woman with her first. Are you Mr Hobson?

JIM (*quickly*): Certainly not. I'm not ill.

DOCTOR: Hum. Not much to choose between you. You've both got your fate written on your faces.

JIM: Do you mean that I—?

DOCTOR: I mean he has and you will.

HOBSON: Doctor, will you attend to me?

DOCTOR: Yes. Now, sir. (*He sits by him and holds his wrist.*)

HOBSON: I've never been in a bad way before this morning. Never wanted a doctor in my life.

DOCTOR: You've needed. But you've not sent.

HOBSON: But this morning—

DOCTOR: I ken – well.

HOBSON: What! You know!

DOCTOR: Any fool would ken.

HOBSON: Eh?

DOCTOR: Any fool but one fool and that's yourself.

HOBSON: You're damned polite.

DOCTOR: If ye want flattery, I dare say ye can get it from your friend. I'm giving you ma medical opinion.

HOBSON: I want your opinion on my complaint, not on my character.

DOCTOR: Your complaint and your character are the same.

HOBSON: Then you'll kindly separate them and you'll tell me—

DOCTOR (*rising and taking up hat*): I'll tell you nothing, sir. I don't diagnose as my patients wish, but as my intellect and sagacity direct. Good morning to you.

JIM: But you have not diagnosed.

DOCTOR: Sir, if I am to interview a patient in the presence of a third party, the least that third party can do is to keep his mouth shut.

JIM: After that, there's only one thing for it. He shifts or I do.

HOBSON: You'd better go, Jim.

JIM: There are other doctors, Henry.

HOBSON: I'll keep this one. I've got to teach him a lesson. Scotchmen can't come over Salford lads this road.

JIM: If that's it, I'll leave you.

HOBSON: That's it. I can bully as well as a foreigner.

    JIM *goes out.*

DOCTOR: That's better, Mr Hobson. (*He puts hat down.*)

HOBSON: If I'm better, you've not had much to do with it.

DOCTOR: I think my calculated rudeness—

HOBSON: If you calculate your fees at the same rate as your rudeness, they'll be high.

DOCTOR: I calculate by time, Mr Hobson, so we'd better get to business. Will you unbutton your shirt?

HOBSON (*doing it*): No hanky-panky now.

DOCTOR (*ignoring his remark and examining*): Aye. It just confirms ma first opinion. Ye've had a breakdown this A.M.?

HOBSON: You might say so.

DOCTOR: Melancholic? Depressed?

HOBSON (*buttoning shirt*): Question was whether the razor would beat me, or I'd beat razor. I won, that time. The razor's in the yard. But I'll never dare to try shaving myself again.

DOCTOR: And do you seriously require me to tell you the cause, Mr Hobson?

HOBSON: I'm paying thee brass to tell me.

DOCTOR: Chronic alcoholism, if you know what that means.

HOBSON: Aye.

DOCTOR: A serious case.

HOBSON: I know it's serious. What do you think you're here for? It isn't to tell me something I know already. It's to cure me.

DOCTOR: Very well. I will write you a prescription. (*Produces notebook. Sits at table and writes with copying pencil.*)

HOBSON: Stop that!

DOCTOR: I beg your pardon.

HOBSON: I won't take it. None of your druggist's muck for me. I'm particular about what I put into my stomach.

DOCTOR: Mr Hobson, if you don't mend your manners, I'll certify you for a lunatic asylum. Are you aware that you've drunk yourself within six months of the grave? You'd a warning this morning that any sane man would listen to and you're going to listen to it, sir.

HOBSON: By taking your prescription?

DOCTOR: Precisely. You will take this mixture, Mr Hobson, and you will practise total abstinence for the future.

HOBSON: You ask me to give up my reasonable refreshment!

DOCTOR: I forbid alcohol absolutely.

HOBSON: Much use your forbidding is. I've had my liquor for as long as I remember, and I'll have it to the end. If I'm to be beaten by beer I'll die fighting, and I'm none practising unnatural teetotalism for the sake of lengthening out my unalcoholic days. Life's got to be worth living before I'll live it.

DOCTOR (*rising and taking hat again*): If that's the way you talk, my services are of no use to you.

HOBSON: They're not. I'll pay you on the nail for this. (*Rising and sorting money from pocket.*)

DOCTOR: I congratulate you on the impulse, Mr Hobson.

HOBSON: Nay, it's a fair deal, doctor. I've had value. You've been a tonic to me. When I got up I never thought to see the 'Moonraker's' again, but I'm ready for my early morning draught this minute. (*Holds out money.*)

DOCTOR (*putting hat down, moving to Hobson and talking earnestly*): Man, will ye no be warned? Ye pig-headed animal, alcohol is poison to ye, deadly, virulent with a system in the state yours is.

HOBSON: You're getting warm about it. Will you take your fee? (*Holding out money.*)

DOCTOR: Yes. When I've earned it. Put it in your pocket, Mr Hobson. I hae na finished with ye yet.

HOBSON: I thought you had.

DOCTOR: Do ye ken that ye're defying me? Ye'll die fighting, will ye? Aye, it's a gay, high-sounding sentiment, ma mannie, but ye'll no dae it, do ye hear? Ye'll no slip from me now. I've got ma grip on ye. Ye'll die sober, and ye'll live the longest time ye can before ye die. Have ye a wife, Mr Hobson?

  HOBSON *points upward.*

In bed?

HOBSON: Higher than that.

DOCTOR: It's a pity. A man like you should keep a wife handy.

HOBSON: I'm not so partial to women.

DOCTOR: Women are a necessity, sir. Have ye no female relative that can manage ye?

HOBSON: Manage?

DOCTOR: Keep her thumb firm on ye?

HOBSON: I've got three daughters, Doctor MacFarlane, and they tried to keep their thumbs on me.

DOCTOR: Well? Where are they?

HOBSON: Married – and queerly married.

DOCTOR: You drove them to it.

HOBSON: They all grew uppish. Maggie worst of all.

DOCTOR: Maggie? Then I'll tell ye what ye'll do, Mr Hobson.

You will get Maggie back. At any price. At all costs to your
pride, as your medical man I order you to get Maggie back.
I don't know Maggie, but I prescribe her, and – damn ye,
sir, are ye going to defy me again!

HOBSON: I tell you I won't have it.

DOCTOR: You'll have to have it. You're a dunderheaded lump
of obstinacy, but I've taken a fancy to ye and I decline to let
ye kill yeself.

HOBSON: I've escaped from the thraldom of women once,
and—

DOCTOR: And a pretty mess you've made of your liberty.
Now this Maggie ye mention – if ye'll tell me where she's
to be found, I'll just step round and have a crack with her
maself, for I've gone beyond the sparing of a bit of trouble
over ye.

HOBSON: You'll waste your time.

DOCTOR: I'll cure you, Mr Hobson.

HOBSON: She won't come back.

DOCTOR: Oh. Now that's a possibility. If she's a sensible body
I concur with your opinion she'll no come back, but women
are a soft-hearted race and she'll maybe take pity on ye after
all.

HOBSON: I want no pity.

DOCTOR: If she's the woman that I take her for ye'll get no
pity. Ye'll get discipline.

> HOBSON *rises and tries to speak.*

Don't interrupt me, sir. I'm talking.

HOBSON: I've noticed it. (*Sits.*)

DOCTOR: You asked me for a cure, and Maggie's the name of
the cure you need. Maggie, sir, do you hear? Maggie!

> *Enter* MAGGIE *in outdoor clothes.*

MAGGIE: What about me?

DOCTOR (*staggered, then*): Are you Maggie!

MAGGIE: I'm Maggie.

DOCTOR: Ye'll do.

HOBSON (*getting his breath*): What are you doing under my roof?

MAGGIE: I've come because I was fetched.

HOBSON: Who fetched you?

MAGGIE: Tubby Wadlow.

HOBSON (*rising*): Tubby can quit my shop this minute.

DOCTOR (*putting him back*): Sit down, Mr Hobson.

MAGGIE: He said you're dangerously ill.

DOCTOR: He is. I'm Doctor MacFarlane. Will you come and live here again?

MAGGIE: I'm married.

DOCTOR: I know that, Mrs—

MAGGIE: Mossop.

DOCTOR: Your father's drinking himself to death, Mrs Mossop.

HOBSON: Look here, Doctor, what's passed between you and me isn't for everybody's ears.

DOCTOR: I judge your daughter's not the sort to want the truth wrapped round with a feather-bed for fear it hits her hard.

MAGGIE (*nodding appreciatively*): Go on. I'd like to hear it all.

HOBSON: Just nasty-minded curiosity.

DOCTOR: I don't agree with you, Mr Hobson. If Mrs Mossop is to sacrifice her own home to come to you, she's every right to know the reason why.

HOBSON: Sacrifice! If you saw her home you'd find another word than that. Two cellars in Oldfield Road.

MAGGIE: I'm waiting, Doctor.

DOCTOR: I've a constitutional objection to seeing patients slip through ma fingers when it's avoidable, Mrs Mossop, and I'll do ma best for your father, but ma medicine willna do him any good without your medicine to back me up. He needs a tight hand on him all the time.

MAGGIE: I've not same chance I had before I married.

DOCTOR: Ye'll have no chance at all unless ye come and live

here. I willna talk about the duty of a daughter because I
doubt he's acted badly by ye, but on the broad grounds of
humanity, it's saving life if ye'll come—

MAGGIE: I might.

DOCTOR: Nay, but will ye?

MAGGIE: You've told me what you think. The rest's my
business.

HOBSON: That's right, Maggie. (*To Doctor.*) That's what you
get for interfering with folks' private affairs. So now you
can go, with your tail between your legs, Doctor
MacFarlane.

DOCTOR: On the contrary, I am going, Mr Hobson, with the
profound conviction that I leave you in excellent hands.
One prescription is on the table, Mrs Mossop. The other
two are total abstinence and – you.

MAGGIE (*nodding amiably*): Good morning.

DOCTOR: Good morning.

  Exit DOCTOR. MAGGIE *picks up prescription and follows
  to door.*

MAGGIE: Tubby!

  She stands by door, TUBBY *just enters inside it.*
Go round to Oldfield Road and ask my husband to come
here and get this made up at Hallow's on your way back.

TUBBY: Yes, Miss – Mrs Mossop.

MAGGIE: Tell Mr Mossop that I want him quick.

  TUBBY *nods and goes.*

HOBSON: Maggie, you know I can't be an abstainer. A man
of my habits. At my time of life.

MAGGIE: You can if I come here to make you.

HOBSON: Are you coming?

MAGGIE: I don't know yet. I haven't asked my husband.

HOBSON: You ask Will Mossop! Maggie, I'd better thoughts
of you. Making an excuse like that to me. If you want to
come you'll come so what Will Mossop says, and well you
know it.

MAGGIE: I don't want to come, father. I expect no holiday existence here with you to keep in health. But if Will tells me it's my duty I shall come.

HOBSON: You know as well as I do asking Will's a matter of form.

MAGGIE: Matter of form! My husband a matter of form! He's the—

HOBSON: I dare say, but he is not the man that wears the breeches at your house.

MAGGIE: My husband's my husband, father, so whatever else he is. And my home's my home and all, and what you said of it now to Doctor MacFarlane's a thing you'll pay for. It's no gift to a married woman to come back to the home she's shut of.

HOBSON: Look here, Maggie, you're talking straight and I'll talk straight and all. When I'm set I'm set. You're coming here. I didn't want you when that doctor said it, but, by gum, I want you now. It's been my daughters' hobby crossing me. Now you'll come and look after me.

MAGGIE: All of us?

HOBSON: No. Not all of you. You're eldest.

MAGGIE: There's another man with claims on me.

HOBSON: I'll give him claims. Aren't I your father?

    ALICE *enters. She is rather elaborately dressed for so early in the day, and languidly haughty.*

MAGGIE: And I'm not your only daughter.

ALICE: You been here long, Maggie?

MAGGIE: A while.

ALICE: Ah, well, a fashionable solicitor's wife doesn't rise so early as the wife of a working cobbler. You'd be up when Tubby came.

MAGGIE: A couple of hours earlier.

ALICE: You're looking all right, father. You've quite a colour.

HOBSON: I'm very ill.

MAGGIE: He's not so well, Alice. The doctor says one of us must come and live here to look after him.

ALICE: I live in the Crescent myself.

MAGGIE: I've heard it was that way on. Somebody's home will have to go.

ALICE: I don't think I can be expected to come back to this after what I've been used to lately.

HOBSON: Alice!

ALICE: Well, I say it ought to be Maggie, father. She's the eldest.

HOBSON: And I say you're—

What she is we don't learn, as VICKEY *enters effectively and goes effusively to Hobson.*

VICKEY: Father, you're ill! (*Embracing him.*)

HOBSON: Vickey! My baby! At last I find a daughter who cares for me.

VICKEY: Of course I care. Don't the others? (*Releasing herself from his grasp.*)

HOBSON: You will live with me, Vickey, won't you?

VICKEY: What? (*She stands away from him.*)

MAGGIE: One of us is needed to look after him.

VICKEY: Oh, but it can't be me. In my circumstances, Maggie!

MAGGIE: What circumstances?

ALICE: Don't you know?

MAGGIE: No.

VICKEY *whispers to Maggie.*

HOBSON: What's the matter? What are you all whispering about?

MAGGIE: Father, don't you think you ought to put a collar on before Will comes?

HOBSON: Put a collar on for Will Mossop? There's something wrong with your sense of proportion, my girl.

VICKEY: You're always pretending to folk about your husband, Maggie, but you needn't keep it up with us. We know Will here.

MAGGIE: Father, either I can go home or you can go and put a collar on for Will. I'll have him treated with respect.

ALICE: I expect you'd put a collar on in any case, father.

HOBSON (*rising*): Of course I should. I'm going to put a collar on. But understand me, Maggie, it's not for the sake of Will Mossop. It's because my neck is cold.

Exit HOBSON.

MAGGIE: Now, then, which of us is it to be?

VICKEY: It's no use looking at me like that, Maggie. I've told you I'm expecting.

MAGGIE: I don't see that that rules you out. It might happen to any of us.

ALICE: Maggie!

MAGGIE: What's the matter? Children do happen to married women, and we're all married.

ALICE: Well, I'm not going to break my home up and that's flat.

VICKEY: My child comes first with me.

MAGGIE: I see. You've got a house of furniture, and you've got a child coming, so father can drink himself to death for you.

ALICE: That's not fair speaking. I'd come if there were no one else. You know very well it's your duty, Maggie.

VICKEY: Duty? I should think it 'ud be a pleasure to live here after a year or two in cellars.

MAGGIE: I've had thirty years of the pleasure of living with father, thanks.

ALICE: Do you mean to say you won't come?

MAGGIE: It isn't for me to say at all. It's for my husband.

VICKEY: Oh, do stop talking about your husband. If Alice and I don't need to ask our husbands, I'm sure you never need ask yours. Will Mossop hasn't the spirit of a louse and we know it as well as you do.

MAGGIE: Maybe Will's come on since you saw him, Vickey.

It's getting a while ago. There he is now in the shop. I'll go
and put it to him.

Exit MAGGIE.

VICKEY: Stop her! (*Going to door.*)

ALICE (*detaining her*): Let her do it in her own way. I'm not
coming back here.

VICKEY: Nor me.

ALICE: There's only Maggie for it.

VICKEY: Yes. But we've got to be careful, Alice. She mustn't
have things too much her way.

ALICE: It's our way as well, isn't it?

VICKEY: Not coming is our way. But when she's with him
alone and we're not— (*Stopping.*)

ALICE: Yes.

VICKEY: Can't you see what I'm thinking, Alice? It is so
difficult to say. Suppose poor father gets worse and they are
here, Maggie and Will, and you and I – out of sight and out
of mind. Can't you see what I mean?

ALICE: He might leave them his money?

VICKEY: That would be most unfair to us.

ALICE: Father must make his will at once. Albert shall draw
it up.

VICKEY: That's it, Alice. And don't let's leave Maggie too long
with Will. She's only telling him what to say, and then she'll
pretend he thought of it himself. (*She opens door.*) Why,
Will, what are you doing up the ladder?

WILLIE (*off*): I'm looking over the stock.

VICKEY (*indignantly*): It's father's stock, not yours.

WILLIE: That's so. But if I'm to come into a thing I like to
know what I'm coming into.

ALICE: That's never Willie Mossop.

VICKEY (*still by door*): Are you coming into this?

    WILL *enters.* MAGGIE *follows him. He is not aggressive, but
he is prosperous and has self-confidence. Against Alice and Vickey
he is consciously on his mettle.*

WILLIE: That's the proposal, isn't it?

VICKEY: I didn't know it was.

WILLIE: Now, then, Maggie, go and bring your father down and be sharp. I'm busy at my shop, so what they are at his.

   MAGGIE *takes Will's hat off and puts it on settee, then exits.*

   It's been a good business in its day, too, has Hobson's.

ALICE: What on earth do you mean? It's a good business still.

WILLIE: You try to sell it, and you'd learn. Stock and goodwill 'ud fetch about two hundred.

VICKEY: Don't talk so foolish, Will. Two hundred for a business like father's!

WILLIE: Two hundred as it is. Not as it was in our time, Vickey.

ALICE: Do you mean to tell me father isn't rich?

WILLIE: If you'd not married into the law you'd know what they think of your father today in trading circles. Vickey ought to know. Her husband's in trade.

VICKEY (*indignantly*): My Fred in trade!

WILLIE: Isn't he?

VICKEY: He's in the wholesale. That's business, not trade. And the value of father's shop is no affair of yours, Will Mossop.

WILLIE: Now I thought maybe it was. If Maggie and me are coming here—

VICKEY: You're coming to look after father.

WILLIE: Maggie can do that with one hand tied behind her back. I'll look after the business.

ALICE: You'll do what's arranged for you.

WILLIE: I'll do the arranging, Alice. If we come here, we come here on my terms.

VICKEY: They'll be fair terms.

WILLIE: I'll see they're fair to me and Maggie.

ALICE: Will Mossop, do you know who you're talking to?

WILLIE: Aye. My wife's young sisters. Times have changed a bit since you used to order me about this shop, haven't they, Alice?

ALICE: Yes. I'm Mrs Albert Prosser now.

WILLIE: So you are, to outsiders. And you'd be surprised the number of people that call me Mr Mossop now. We do get on in the world, don't we?

VICKEY: Some folks get on too fast.

WILLIE: It's a matter of opinion. I know Maggie and me gave both of you a big leg up when we arranged your marriage portions, but I dunno that we're grudging you the sudden lift you got.

Enter HOBSON *and* MAGGIE.

WILLIE: Good morning, father. I'm sorry to hear you're not so well.

HOBSON: I'm a changed man, Will. (*He comes down and sits on arm-chair.*)

WILLIE: There used to be room for improvement.

HOBSON: What! (*He starts up.*)

MAGGIE: Sit down, father.

WILLIE: Aye. Don't let us be too long about this. You've kept me waiting now a good while and my time's valuable. I'm busy at my shop.

HOBSON: Is your shop more important than my life?

WILLIE: That's a bit like asking if a pound of tea weighs heavier than a pound of lead. I'm worried about your life because it worrits Maggie, but I'm none worrited that bad I'll see my business suffer for the sake of you.

HOBSON: This isn't what I've a right to expect from you, Will.

WILLIE: You've no *right* to expect I care whether you sink or swim.

MAGGIE: Will.

WILLIE: What's to do? You told me to take a high hand, didn't you?

ALICE: And we're to stay here and watch Maggie and Will abusing father when he's ill.

WILLIE: No need for you to stay.

HOBSON: That's a true word, Will Mossop.

VICKEY: Father! You take his side against your flesh and blood.

HOBSON: That doesn't come too well from you, my girl. Neither of you would leave your homes to come to care for me. You're not for me, so you're against me.

ALICE: We're not against you, father. We want to stay and see that Will deals fairly by you.

HOBSON: Oh, I'm not capable of looking after myself, amn't I? I've to be protected by you girls lest I'm over-reached, and over-reached by whom? By Willie Mossop! I may be ailing, but I've fight enough left in me for a dozen such as him, and if you're thinking that the manhood's gone from me, you can go and think it somewhere else than in my house.

VICKEY: But father – dear father—

HOBSON: I'm not so dear to you if you'd to think twice about coming here to do for me, let alone jibbing at it the way you did. A proper daughter would have jumped – aye, skipped like a calf by the cedars of Lebanon – at the thought of being helpful to her father.

ALICE: Did Maggie skip?

HOBSON: She's a bit ancient for skipping exercise, is Maggie; but she's coming round to reconcilement with the thought of living here, and that is more than you are doing, Alice, isn't it? Eh? Are you willing to come?

ALICE (sullenly): No.

HOBSON: Or you, Vickey?

VICKEY: It's my child, father. I—

HOBSON: Never mind what it is. Are you coming or not?

VICKEY. No.

HOBSON: Then you that aren't willing can leave me to talk with them that are.

ALICE: Do you mean that we're to go?

HOBSON: I understand you've homes to go to.

ALICE: Oh, father!

HOBSON: Open the door for them, Will.

WILL *rises, crosses, and opens door.* ALICE *and* VICKEY *stare in silent anger. Then* ALICE *sweeps to her gloves on the table.*

ALICE: Vickey!

ALICE *moves on towards door.*

VICKEY: Well, I don't know!

MAGGIE (*from her chair by the fire-place*): We'll be glad to see you here at tea-time on a Sunday afternoon if you'll condescend to come sometimes.

VICKEY: Beggars on horseback.

VICKEY *and* ALICE *pass out.*

WILL (*closing door*): Nay, come, there's no ill-will. (*He returns to table and sits.*)

HOBSON: Now, my lad, I'll tell you what I'll do.

WILLIE: Aye, we can come to grips better now there are no fine ladies about.

HOBSON: They've got stiff necks with pride, and the difference between you two and them's a thing I ought to mark and that I'm going to mark. There's times for holding back and times for letting loose, and being generous. Now, you're coming here, to this house, both of you, and you can have the back bedroom for your own and the use of this room split along with me. Maggie 'ull keep house, and if she's time to spare she can lend a hand in the shop. I'm finding Will a job. You can come back to your old bench in the cellar, Will, and I'll pay you the old wage of eighteen shillings a week and you and me 'ull go equal whacks in the cost of the housekeeping, and if that's not handsome, I dunno what is. I'm finding you a house rent free and paying half the keep of your wife.

WILLIE: Come home, Maggie. (*He rises.*)

MAGGIE: I think I'll have to. (*She rises.*)

HOBSON: Whatever's the hurry for?

WILLIE: It may be news to you, but I've a business round in Oldfield Road and I'm neglecting it with wasting my time here.

HOBSON: Wasting time? Maggie, what's the matter with Will? I've made him a proposal.

WILL *is by door.*

MAGGIE: He's a shop of his own to see to, father.

HOBSON (*incredulous*): A man who's offered a job at Hobson's doesn't want to worry with a shop of his own in a wretched cellar in Oldfield Road.

WILLIE: Shall I tell him, Maggie, or shall we go?

HOBSON: Go! I don't want to keep a man who— (*Rises.*)

MAGGIE: If he goes, I go with him, father. You'd better speak out, Will.

WILLIE: All right, I will. We've been a year in yon wretched cellar and do you know what we've done? We've paid off Mrs Hepworth what she lent us for our start and made a bit o' brass on top o' that. We've got your high-class trade away from you. That shop's a cellar, and as you say, it's wretched, but they come to us in it, and they don't come to you. Your trade's gone down till all you sell is clogs. You've got no trade, and me and Maggie's got it all and now you're on your bended knees to her to come and live with you, and all you think to offer me is my old job at eighteen shillings a week. Me that's the owner of a business that is starving yours to death.

HOBSON: But – but – you're Will Mossop, you're my old shoe hand.

WILLIE: Aye. I were, but I've moved on a bit since then. Your daughter married me and set about my education. And – and now I'll tell you what I'll do and it'll be the handsome thing and all from me to you. I'll close my shop—

HOBSON: Oh! That doesn't sound like doing so well.

WILLIE: I'm doing well, but I'll do better here. I'll transfer to this address and what I'll do that's generous is this: I'll take you into partnership and give you your half-share on the condition you're sleeping partner and you don't try interference on with me.

HOBSON: A partner! You – here—

WILLIE: William Mossop, late Hobson, is the name this shop 'ull have.

MAGGIE: Wait a bit, Will. I don't agree to that.

HOBSON: Oh, so you have piped up at last. I began to think you'd both lost your senses together.

MAGGIE: It had better not be 'late Hobson'.

WILLIE: Well, I meant it should.

HOBSON: Just wait a bit. I want to know if I'm taking this in aright. I'm to be given a half-share in my own business on condition I take no part in running it. Is that what you said?

WILLIE: That's it.

HOBSON: Well, I've heard of impudence before, but—

MAGGIE: It's all right, father.

HOBSON: But did you hear what he said?

MAGGIE: Yes. That's settled. Quite settled, father. It's only the name we're arguing about. (*To Will.*) I won't have 'late Hobson's', Will.

HOBSON: I'm not dead, yet, my lad, and I'll show you I'm not.

MAGGIE: I think Hobson and Mossop is best.

HOBSON: His name on my sign-board!

WILLIE: The best I'll do is this: Mossop and Hobson.

MAGGIE: No.

WILLIE: Mossop and Hobson or it's Oldfield Road for us, Maggie.

MAGGIE: Very well. Mossop and Hobson.

HOBSON: But—

WILLIE (*opening door and looking through*): I'll make some alterations in this shop, and all. I will so. (*He goes through door and returns at once with a battered cane chair.*)

HOBSON: Alterations in my shop!

WILLIE: In mine. Look at that chair. How can you expect the high-class customers to come and sit on a chair like that? Why, we'd only a cellar, but they did sit on cretonne for their trying on.

HOBSON: Cretonne! It's pampering folk.

WILLIE: Cretonne for a cellar, and morocco for this shop. Folk like to be pampered. Pampering pays. (*He takes the chair out and returns immediately.*) There'll be a carpet on that floor, too.

HOBSON: Carpet! Morocco! Young man, do you think this shop is in Saint Ann's Square, Manchester?

WILLIE: Not yet. But it is going to be.

HOBSON: What does he mean? (*Appealing to heaven.*)

WILLIE: It's no farther from Chapel Street to Saint Ann's Square than it is from Oldfield Road to Chapel Street. I've done one jump in a year and if I wait a bit I'll do the other. Maggie, I reckon your father could do with a bit of fresh air after this. I dare say it's come sudden to him. Suppose you walk with him to Albert Prosser's office and get Albert to draw up the deed of partnership.

HOBSON (*looking pathetically first at Maggie, then at Willie, rising obediently*): I'll go and get my hat.

Exit HOBSON.

WILLIE: He's crushed-like, Maggie. I'm afraid I bore on him too hard.

MAGGIE: You needn't be.

WILLIE: I said such things to him, and they sounded as if I meant them, too.

MAGGIE: Didn't you?

WILLIE: Did I? Yes ... I suppose I did. That's just the worst ... from me to him. You told me to be strong and use the power that's come to me through you, but he's the old master, and—

MAGGIE: And you're the new.

WILLIE: Master of Hobson's! It's an outrageous big idea. Did I sound confident, Maggie?

MAGGIE: You did all right.

WILLIE: Eh, but I weren't by half so certain as I sounded. Words came from my mouth that made me jump at my own boldness, and when it came to facing you about the name, I tell you I fair trembled in my shoes. I was carried away like, or I'd not have dared to cross you, Maggie.

MAGGIE: Don't spoil it, Will. (*Moves to him.*) You're the man I've made you and I'm proud.

WILLIE: Thy pride is not in same street, lass, with the pride I have in you. And that reminds me. I've a job to see to.

MAGGIE: What job?

WILLIE: Oh – about the improvements.

MAGGIE: You'll not do owt without consulting me.

WILLIE: I'll do this, lass. (*Goes to and takes her hand.*)

MAGGIE: What are you doing? You leave my wedding ring alone. (*Wrenches hand free.*)

WILLIE: You've worn a brass one long enough.

MAGGIE: I'll wear that ring for ever, Will.

WILLIE: I was for getting you a proper one, Maggie.

MAGGIE: I'm not preventing you. I'll wear your gold for show, but that brass stays where you put it, Will, and if we get too rich and proud we'll just sit down together quiet and and take a long look at it, so as we'll not forget the truth about ourselves. . . . Eh, lad! (*She touches him affectionately.*)

WILL: Eh, lass! (*He kisses her.*)

Enter HOBSON *with his hat on.*

MAGGIE: Ready, father. Come along to Albert's.

HOBSON (*meekly*): Yes, Maggie.

MAGGIE *and* HOBSON *cross below* Will *and go out.* WILL *comes down with amazement, triumph and incredulity written on his face, and attempts to express the inexpressible by saying—*

WILL: Well, by gum! (*He turns to follow the others.*)

CURTAIN

NOTES

Hobson's Choice: The point of the title becomes clear at the
end, when Hobson has no choice at all. The expression
comes from a Hobson who kept horses for hire in Cambridge,
where he claimed to offer a choice of mounts but told the
hirer which to choose he must have.

p. 6   *hump added to nature:* the bustle, a padding or curved framework
worn at the back just below the waist, was intended to
accentuate the figure and cause the folds of the long skirt to
hang gracefully.

p. 12   *John Bright himself:* John Bright (1811–86) was one of the
greatest of Liberal statesmen, with a reputation as an orator.
He was specially honoured in Lancashire, for he came from
Rochdale, and he became the champion of Free Trade, on
which the prosperity of Lancashire industry was founded.

p. 33   *Flat Iron Market:* a second-hand market in Salford.

p. 49   *Manchester Guardian:* Founded as a daily in 1855, it grew far
beyond the status of a local paper under the editorship of
C. P. Scott (1872–1929). In Brighouse's early days it was
one of the glories of Manchester. Since 1959 it has dropped
the 'Manchester' and become gradually more and more a
London publication.

p. 71   *Shut of:* Free of.